Newsroom Buddies

Also by Sandi Latimer
Poodle Mistress: The Autobiographical Story of Life with Nine Toy Poodles

Also by John Kady
A Sentry's Saga on Okinawa
From Kennedy to Kent State: A Reporter's Notebook

Newsroom Buddies

A Working Friendship at
United Press International

Sandi Latimer
and
John Kady

iUniverse LLC
Bloomington

NEWSROOM BUDDIES
A WORKING FRIENDSHIP AT UNITED PRESS INTERNATIONAL

iUniverse books may be ordered through booksellers or by contacting:

iUniverse
1663 Liberty Drive
Bloomington, IN 47403
www.iuniverse.com
1-800-Authors (1-800-288-4677)

Because of the dynamic nature of the Internet, any web addresses or links contained in this book may have changed since publication and may no longer be valid. The views expressed in this work are solely those of the author and do not necessarily reflect the views of the publisher, and the publisher hereby disclaims any responsibility for them.

Any people depicted in stock imagery provided by Thinkstock are models, and such images are being used for illustrative purposes only.
Certain stock imagery © Thinkstock.

ISBN: 978-1-4917-2839-0 (sc)
ISBN: 978-1-4917-2838-3 (e)

Library of Congress Control Number: 2014905310

Printed in the United States of America.

iUniverse rev. date: 05/05/2014

To Patti and Red, our spouses. Thanks for putting up with us throughout our UPI careers and beyond. And to Joyce, who left us way too soon.

Contents

Book 3: 1990–Today

Acknowledgments

While listening to a speech by Jeffrey Zaslow, I had an idea about a statement he made as he talked about the book *The Girls from Ames*. He said men don't have the relationships that women do.

I thought back to forty-two years earlier when John Kady called to offer me a job with United Press International in Columbus, Ohio. I didn't know who he was, and he only knew slightly more about me because I was on his stringer list. What I knew of United Press International was through my journalism training and broadcast jobs.

I looked into his offer, went for an interview and writing test, and eventually started working for him, or with him, as we did many days during the next twenty-two and a half years.

After Zaslow's presentation, I had the opportunity to speak with him for a few minutes and told him about a relationship between a boss and employee that has lasted longer than many marriages. He challenged me to write the story.

John and I began reaching into our memories, going as far back as the days we decided to become journalists. We talked with some of our former coworkers and researched events we covered. We checked books written by our colleagues—*Down to the Wire* and *Unipress*—to confirm the order of the financial problems we all encountered.

I'd like to thank Jeffrey Zaslow for giving us the idea to collaborate on the story you are about to read. Rest in peace, Jeffrey, knowing you inspired some works.

Thanks also to members of the Ohio Writers Guild, with whom John and I met weekly and who listened to some of our story and offered their feedback.

Special thanks go to former Unipressers Ron Cohen, coauthor of *Down to the Wire*, and Tom Foty, now at CBS Radio News, for reading our effort to make sure we had the events in order; and to former UPI staffer Bill Clayton for a photo of a typewriter like we used.

To longtime friend Judith Rogers, thanks for her expertise in editing and guidance, not to mention the ideas that sprouted over the many breakfasts and lunches we shared.

Throughout our reminiscing, John and I shared some good times, and some not so good. We laughed at some incidents about which we wrote, and nearly cried at others.

I hope you enjoy the stories that John and I have so lovingly compiled of a forty-five-year friendship that began with his offering me a job. That friendship took us on a roller-coaster ride through the good days and those not so good at a once great wire service, and then we continued our friendship as we walked a different pathway together again.

—Sandi Latimer

Book I

Photo courtesy of Bill Clayton, a former UPI staffer in
Oklahoma City, Austin, Houston, Dallas, and Washington

1967–1968

Chapter 1

Sandi
Spring 2012
A Get-Together

In the spring of 2012, three of my former coworkers and I gathered around a table at Panera's on the east side of Columbus, Ohio, sipping coffee and nibbling on pastries while sharing stories and laughing.

David Harding started telling how his mother taught him that adding blessed holy water to another amount of water makes the other amount holy.

"When I was in the navy, I had a bottle of water I carried with me when I visited Rome and had it blessed by the Pope," he said. "I saved that bottle of water. When I got to the Pacific, I dumped the blessed water into the ocean. 'Mom,' I told her, 'the whole Pacific is now holy water.'"

John Kady and I had heard David tell that story a couple of weeks earlier when the three of us went to the thoroughbred racetrack at Beulah Park in nearby Grove City and then had cake and iced tea when we dropped John at his house. The story was new for Lee Leonard. All three of us laughed hard at David's story.

I glanced around the room. Not many people were there at that hour—midmorning was too late for breakfast and too early for lunch but just a perfect time for some former coworkers to gather and remember. And laugh.

Stories kept coming, and eventually got around to days at work. Some were funny; some weren't.

"I remember one bad day," I began. "I'd been given a feature day and had set up my own fam tour in Chillicothe. I get home and find a message from John on my answering machine."

John, David, Lee, and I worked for United Press International in Columbus from the late 1960s to 1990. John had been what we called our fearless leader—serving as the bureau manager and state editor during much of his twenty-six years at UPI in Columbus. Lee anchored the Statehouse coverage since his arrival in 1969 until the end of 1990.

David and I worked in the UPI office much of the time, but we each had our turn with Lee for a session of the legislature.

The particular day I was talking about was in 1984. I had a day where I could do whatever I wanted, and I usually went looking for feature stories. Since 1970, I had been writing feature stories that were being used in nearly every newspaper we served in Ohio. In the early 1980s, in order to seek out stories, do interviews, and write the stories, I had a feature day about once a month.

Not wanting to abuse a privilege no one else had, I always came up with a story. That day I had been in touch with a tourism leader in Chillicothe, Ohio's first capital, as I planned to write some summer travel and tourism stories. I scheduled my personal fam tour—familiarization tour of a given area.

I had been escorted through the small city two counties south of Columbus, through an outlet store for kitchenware, and to a small frame building on the outskirts of town, whose chenille bedspreads and iridescent globes on pedestals announced it as a tourist stop. Inside, in addition to the usual knickknacks that people buy as a remembrance of where they've been, were porcelain dolls in elegant gowns. Dolls were made in another part of the building, dressed in handmade outfits, and advertised in *Vogue* magazine.

Now that's a story, I decided on the spot, and began asking questions, taking notes, planning a story I would be sending out to our clients before Mother's Day.

My host was surprised at my wanting to write about a small piece of a historic area when no other travel and tourism writers did it. I always looked for the unusual.

I arrived home in late afternoon and checked the answering machine. I was surprised by the content of the message from John. He sounded serious, not his usual jovial conversational voice.

"Sandi. This is John. Don't cash your paycheck."

I knew UPI was having financial problems—had been for years. The thousand or so employees worldwide kept churning out well-written stories and quality photographs for both print and broadcast outlets. Our pay was comparable with our competitors, whom we often outwrote. And the checks were always on schedule. That's why I was surprised that day.

Bankruptcy soon crept into our vocabulary and into our stories. UPI was going downhill, and we didn't want it to. We in Columbus fought it. I know some employees in other bureaus around the country fought the way we did. Our stories were strongly written, but more than good writing was involved. We had our sources, our contacts.

The fight lasted for six years before wholesale layoffs began and the makeup of a once strong and respected worldwide news agency crumbled.

A couple of hours into our kaffeeklatsch, we decided it was time to move on. David and Lee lived on the east side of town, John and I lived west.

A female restaurant employee held the door for us as we made our way to our cars in the parking lot. John, who by now was maneuvering with a walker after suffering a variety of health problems, was riding with me.

"Would you believe the four of us over there worked together for one company some twenty years ago?" I asked the young woman not long out of high school. "The four of us have more than one hundred years' experience with that company." She gave me a look of disbelief.

Even though the company began to unravel in 1990 and moved into a different form, the camaraderie and strong relationships that the employees in Ohio had knit over the years would never unravel.

Chapter 2

Sandi

October 27, 1967

A Missing Person

I pulled on a rust-colored mock turtleneck sweater that blended with the brown stretch slacks. This was the outfit Joe, the fellow I had been dating the past several months, had given me for my birthday a few weeks earlier. Then the phone rang. I took a deep breath and started for the phone.

Don't let it be, I prayed.

I'd had a few dates called off because Joe, a firefighter, had been called in on his day off when a major fire call came in. Since he was the newest on the force in terms of tenure, he'd often stop in to work the radio communications or be on standby. I guess I could say dates "went up in smoke." I was hoping it wouldn't be that again.

My cheerful greeting was answered by a coworker bringing me up-to-date on what he had heard on the streets late that afternoon.

The date was October 27, 1967, in Delaware, Ohio, a university town about thirty miles north of the state capital of Columbus. I was news director and women's director at the town's radio station, WDLR. I was a one-person news operation—gathering, writing, and airing most of the newscasts. When I was out on my morning rounds in the community, Bill Buchanan, the sales manager, read the newscasts I had prepared. I also hosted a thirty-minute early-afternoon talk show, centered mainly on women but also touching on important topics of the community.

"I'll be there in a few minutes," I said half-excitedly, pressing the button in the cradle of the phone, then releasing it and dialing another number.

"Hazel, can you please tell Joe I'm heading over to Blue Limestone? They found a car in the reservoir. I don't know how long I'll be. I'll call when I get a chance. Thanks. Talk to you later."

I hated breaking dates or postponing them. But when you work in the news business and you're the only person available, you go when and where you have to. On the other hand, Joe was working twenty-four hours on, twenty-four hours off, and date nights were whenever we could squeeze in a few hours for a movie or some other activity. He was out feeding the family's horses, the last chore he had before getting ready to pick me up. We had been planning to go to a movie.

When you're young—we were both twenty-four—and trying to get established in a career, you do what you have to. We both understood each other's commitment to our work.

For the past week I had been following the report of a missing young woman from a neighboring community. Rumors had been swirling: That the boyfriend was involved. That she was pregnant. That she had had a flat tire a few days before and the boyfriend fixed it, but the wheel came off on her way home. That the car was in the reservoir. These were only rumors. I couldn't report rumors. No one could prove anything. I listened and started to dig for facts. Being a one-person operation, I hadn't gotten very far.

After hanging up, I grabbed a jacket, a notebook, and my purse, and raced down the steps and into my car. The reservoir was only a few blocks away. I found a place to park, although already a crowd was beginning to gather. I worked my way through the crowd and walked up to the sheriff's deputy. The officer wasn't my favorite person, but I hoped I could get some information from him.

"Hi, Bill. What's up?" I said, wandering around the immediate scene.

"What's up with you?" he returned. I knew I wasn't going to get much from him.

"Hey, you're the one who has something," I said. "What can you tell me?"

"You know about as much as I do. That's why you're here."

The sun was setting when a wrecker hauled a white car out of the water. The back door on the driver's side was open and water poured out. The front window on the driver's side was open. Or was it broken? I wasn't close enough to tell.

I walked around the car as close as I could get. I wanted to get a good look at the license plate. I had written down the license plate number from the sheriff's report. A quick glance told me it was the car of the missing woman. No body was in the car, though.

"The body surfaced, and then we went in for the car," Bill offered as I looked over the car and made several notes. *At least he contributed something*, I thought. *I have to give him credit for that.*

"What condition was the body in?" I asked.

"You'd have to ask the police chief," he said in a voice that told me he wasn't going to tell me anything more.

Was he miffed that he wasn't the lead investigator after he had taken the missing person report on the young woman little more than a week earlier?

"The city's handling it. We're only here to protect the scene."

Sometimes in a small town, the county sheriff and the city police aren't really the best of friends, but when a big case springs up, they have to work together. That's what these two departments had to do that evening. The sheriff's department now had to share with the police the information they had collected during the past week.

"Thanks, Bill," I said. "Catch you later."

I headed down the path toward my car. I was only about four blocks from the police department, which was a block from my apartment. I could park at home, walk over to the police department, get some information, get back to my apartment, make some phone calls, and still have time to go out on our date. At least Joe and I would have something fresh to talk about over pizza and beer.

The police chief was in his little office, a section partitioned off behind the dispatching area that sat behind a counter in the little room in City Hall opposite the city manager's office. Out a door to the left and down a couple of steps is the fire department. I had made that trek many times on my rounds in the thirteen months I had been working at the radio station. I visited the city manager's office, the police department, and the fire department for the morning reports.

Rarely did I see the police chief at the hours I made my rounds, and this was later than usual for him to be on duty. The pressing issue of the day had him staying around.

"Body's gone to the coroner's office," the chief said. A couple of other people were standing at the counter trying to get some information. One was from the local paper, but I didn't recognize the other fellow.

"Who you calling, Sandi?" asked the police captain. He was on duty as the dispatcher that night.

"I've been feeding the Associated Press, United Press International, and the *Dispatch*," I said. As I obtained fresh information in this case the past week, I would call the wire services—AP and UPI—and the *Columbus Dispatch*, the afternoon newspaper in the capital city. I didn't know who was tipping off the *Columbus Citizen-Journal*, the morning paper; perhaps the Delaware paper? And for the work I was doing—known as stringing—I picked up a couple of bucks a call.

The stranger turned to me. "I'm just passing through. You mind if I call AP?" he asked.

I didn't mind. It would take a load off my shoulders, but also a few bucks out of my pocket.

The radio station where I worked was fed by AP, one of the two major wire services in the country. The other wire service was UPI. Both were set up about the same, with offices in major cities. They obtained news from subscribing newspapers and radio and TV stations in addition to the stories generated by their employees and sent them out on the wires. Subscribers paid to get the service.

I walked back to my apartment, mulling over the events of the past hour or so, sort of preparing my conversation with UPI and the *Dispatch*. I called the *Dispatch* first. That was more of a tip because they would be sending a reporter since Delaware was so close. And they wouldn't be publishing until the following afternoon. They'd have plenty of time to assign a reporter and do their own story. Then I called UPI.

After giving my information to the man who answered the phone, I verified my personal information. I had called a few times on small stories and almost daily on this one. I didn't remember anyone I had spoken with, but I knew I hadn't had this guy before. Stringers, trusted reporters who phone in stories worthy of wire-service placement, always give their names, addresses, phone numbers, and social security numbers. That's in case UPI has any questions or follow-up on stories. The most important reason: they would get paid, if only a couple of dollars for a story.

I always had trouble with my name. My last name was Gould. If people saw it in print, they couldn't pronounce it. If they heard it pronounced, they couldn't spell it. I hated that name, but it was the one I had from birth twenty-four years earlier.

"Hey, you got it right," I told the guy when he correctly spelled my name after I had pronounced it.

"I live on a street by that name," he said.

"That street was named for my great-grandfather," I said. "He owned land in that area."

That was my fifteen seconds of fame.

Chapter 3

John
Monday, October 30, 1967
The Woman in Delaware

Monday started as any other Monday. My wife, Joyce, was sipping a cup of coffee as I hung up the phone.

"Why do you always call the office before you go to work?" she yawned.

"I want to get a heads-up on anything that might be happening." I poured a cup of coffee and buttered a couple of slices of toast. "Want one?"

She shook her head and rubbed her eyes.

"Anything happening?" she asked.

"Not really. Just a regular Monday morning," I said, heading to the front door to bring in the *Citizen-Journal*. "Betty wants a cheeseburger."

"A cheeseburger at this hour of the morning?" Joyce wrinkled her nose.

"What would you eat when you finish work?" I wanted to know.

"It seems strange to eat a cheeseburger at six o'clock in the morning," she mused. "Most people want breakfast food. You know, cereal, bacon, and eggs."

Betty was working the third shift at United Press International in downtown Columbus, where I was bureau manager. She'd leave shortly after bringing me up-to-date when I arrived.

I read the paper, making a mental note of some of the stories we might want to use. Suddenly our moment of peace was broken when our two daughters rushed in and gave me a hug.

"You can't go to work without saying good-bye to us," they yelled.

Gretchen was in the first grade and Jennifer in the second. Since I got to work around six o'clock, this was an hour most kids wouldn't be up, but not our girls.

Wanting to show us how big she was, Jennifer poured her own bowl of cereal and carefully added the milk and sugar. She also fixed a bowl for Gretchen, who began gulping down the cereal.

"Slow down, girl," I said. "You'll choke if you keep eating so fast."

"But, Daddy, I gotta get to school to see what my teacher did this weekend," Gretchen said.

"You have plenty of time to get to school," I told her. "Your teacher probably isn't even awake yet. You should go back to bed after I leave."

Meanwhile, Joyce started fixing sandwiches for the girls' lunches. We lived only a few blocks from Prairie Lincoln Elementary School, and the girls insisted they were old enough to walk by themselves.

Going to work as early as I did, I bypassed much of the traffic and the morning rush hour. I stopped at an all-night café down the street from the office to get Betty's cheeseburger. I walked into the UPI office and put the sack containing the cheeseburger and a cup of coffee on the desk in front of her.

"Thanks, John," she said, handing me a five-dollar bill.

"Don't worry about it," I said, refusing it. "I don't have change." The door banged, and in rushed the morning broadcast writer, who plopped down in the chair across the desk from Betty.

"Hey, Jeff," I said. "What's up with you?"

"Bus was running a little late this morning," he said, stuffing his brown-bagged lunch in a bottom drawer before he grabbed the morning's stories he would condense for the broadcast clients.

After hanging up my coat, I sat down at a desk on the other side of the room with the stack of stories that made up the morning's report, checking to see what stories had been written and transmitted to the newspapers that publish in the afternoon, and to the radio and television stations in Ohio. I made a note that we had the story concerning the missing woman whose body and car were found in Delaware on Friday night.

"Anything I should know?" I asked Betty when I returned the stack of stories to her desk.

"It's a normal, quiet Monday," she said, munching on her cheeseburger and sipping her coffee. "What do you need me to cover on Election Day next week?"

That was one thing I had to finalize: who was writing what. With a quiet day ahead, I would have time to do a final check of the major races and make sure everyone had an assignment.

The ringing phones interrupted any thoughts of the election. Radio reporters were calling after their morning rounds to offer us stories that would run for the afternoon newspapers and for the broadcast outlets.

Jeff and I took turns answering the phone calls, making instant decisions about the immediacy and necessity of the story and whether our opponent, AP, would be running it. Occasionally someone would walk in and hand us a news release. Even though we had few calls and visitors at that hour, the time passed quickly.

"Morning, Kady." I looked up and saw Dick Lightner taking off his coat. Dick was working on the rewrite desk today. I could hand off much of the work to him while I concentrated on the upcoming election. The person on rewrite wrote most of the stories in midday, keeping tabs on our neighbor Scripps-Howard Press Service, and checking the afternoon *Columbus Dispatch* when its first edition came in around eleven o'clock.

A little after noon, we were ready to start the next cycle: transmitting stories for the Tuesday morning papers.

"John, you ready for lunch?" Dick asked. I looked at the clock. Nearly one o'clock.

"Yeah, where do you want to go?" I asked.

"Let's go to the Ringside," he said.

We walked out the back door and down the steps into the alley to the little bar, one of the oldest in the city. It was past the normal lunchtime, and we'd be able to get a table and talk.

"You have the election night coverage planned?" Dick asked.

An off-year election was approaching. The presidential election was a year away. A governor's race was three years off. School issues were on the ballot in many districts. Mayors' races were a highlight in many Ohio cities.

I was facing another problem: trying to find new employees. I liked to have a pool of people I could call when someone unexpectedly gave a two-week notice or someone was asked to move to another bureau in the country to fill a vacancy. Times were changing. It wasn't like the previous generation, when someone got a job and held it for life. Here I was: age thirty-four, an Air Force veteran, a college graduate, and on my fourth assignment in less than ten years—although it was for the same company.

"When is Rick expecting to be called up?" Dick asked about one of his coworkers who had been in ROTC in college and was waiting to be called to active duty in the Vietnam War.

"He doesn't know. You know how it is in the army—hurry up and wait," I said, taking a swallow of beer to wash down the hamburger with a large slice of onion. "Do you have any idea of anyone who would want to work with this group?"

Dick didn't think twice.

"I had a call from a woman Friday night on the missing woman case in Delaware," he said. "Seemed like a knowledgeable woman. Had all the pertinent information and background. A lot better than some stringers we talk to."

"Did you get her name and number?" I asked.

"Yeah," he said. "It's in the stringer drawer. Why don't you call her? Sounds like she may be a hot blonde."

"Really?" I asked. "Remember, you're a married man."

"And so are you," Dick came back. "Hey," he said, looking at his watch and gulping down his last swallow of beer. "'Bout time we get back to work. Jeff is gonna want to get out of there pretty soon."

We walked back to the office through the rear entrance.

"You won't forget to call her?" Dick reminded me. "I think her name is Sharon, or something like that. Begins with an S."

"Anything happening, Jeff?" I asked when we returned to the office.

I opened the drawer where the stringer notes were kept. On top was the name of a Sandi Gould of WDLR in Delaware. I made a note with her name and phone number.

The night shift started work at 3:00 p.m., and I had a little bit of free time before I left for the day. I picked up the phone and dialed the number for WDLR.

Chapter 4

Sandi
Monday, October 30, 1967
A Phone Call

Mondays seem to be the slowest days in the news business. That's because most state and local offices where news can be generated are closed on Saturdays and Sundays. By early Monday, everyone is getting started again. Sports takes up much of the space in newspapers and time on radio and TV after weekend action. Much weekend news comes from police, fire, and Highway Patrol reports. At that time in a small town, we didn't have the usual Friday or Saturday night fights that ended in a gunshot. A drug arrest was big news, and so was copper theft.

I'd start the morning with checks in City Hall. When it was Joe's turn to work, I'd join him and his coworkers for coffee at the L&K Restaurant across the street from City Hall and then check with the crew getting off work to see if they'd had any interesting runs since the previous afternoon. I'd walk out through the police department, checking with the captain going off duty and heading home in time to say good-bye to his wife, the city manager's secretary. Generally there wasn't much, but this time I had to get the latest on the investigation into the death of the young woman whose body was found a few days earlier.

If Joe was on the job, I'd skip the restaurant and start rounds at the police station.

When I arrived at the radio station, I'd write stories from what I had gathered that morning, stripping the news off the Associated Press teletype machine to compile newscasts. I'd also type up a little newssheet with the top local, state, national, and international news, and possibly some sports scores, make copies, and distribute them around the downtown business district and check in with business leaders. I shared many of the day's events when I sat down with a cup of coffee at a businessman's table at the famed Bun's Restaurant. Later I learned I was the first woman to join that table. The first day I joined them, no one said I couldn't sit with them.

I'd get back to the station around nine thirty, write stories, and make more phone calls, a routine I had developed when I started at the station.

Monday was my day to have the local extension agent on my program. She gave household hints, recipes, child-rearing tips, decorating ideas, anything she wanted to chat about. I had a few minutes between my show and my 3:00 p.m. newscast, and then I was done for the day.

As I signed off the newscast that day, Bob flipped a switch in the main studio and his voice came over the intercom: "Sandi, the blinking light is for you."

"Good afternoon. This is Sandi. How may I help you?" This was my standard phone greeting that I had created when I worked at the radio station before I joined WDLR in Delaware. I patterned it after one the woman whom I worked with had used. I still use that style of greeting today when I answer the phone at home.

I was glad I was sitting down.

"This is John Kady at UPI in Columbus, and I'd like to have you come to work for us. On rewrite."

"I'm honored. I don't know what to say," I stammered. "May I have your phone number so I can call you back?"

I really didn't know what all he meant when he offered me a position on rewrite. All I knew was that I had been offered a job.

It took me a few minutes to drive home. I changed into jeans and a sweater and drove out to see Joe, who was at his parents' house, taking care of his horses.

"I had a strange phone call this afternoon," I said as we shared coffee and cookies in the kitchen of the rambling ranch-style house. "I was offered a job in Columbus."

"You're going to look into it, aren't you?" he asked.

"I don't know. I've just gotten a good start here these past thirteen months. I feel comfortable with the job and know a few things I want to do yet. I'm not ready for a new job."

I had started from scratch when I began that job, creating a news department as I was learning my way around a new city and meeting people. I was a one-person operation in a small station and one of eight people on staff. It took a while to accomplish something.

I also had the two of us in mind. Could we have a future together? I took another sip of coffee and grabbed a cookie from the plate in the middle of the table.

"You'd be stupid if you don't look into it," Joe said, reaching across the table to hold my shaking hand.

"I will," I said with some reservation.

I don't remember eating dinner that evening. My mind was elsewhere. I had a chance at a bigger job, but did I want to move on? I had recently met with news directors from other small stations in central and north central Ohio, and we had talked about forming some kind of broadcast network. I would have to learn how to incorporate taped interviews into my newscasts. This was something I had been discussing with my station manager.

I still had many things that I wanted to do at the station, where I was developing a respectable news department. But if I moved on, could I do more toward my goal of becoming a baseball announcer? I had set my sights on that career goal at age thirteen and started studying journalism.

UPI had come calling. I was familiar with the AP wires from college and at work and had read the UPI wire when I worked at WBCO in Bucyrus, where I had been before I accepted the job in Delaware. I had never dreamed I would be working for such a big operation as UPI.

I picked up the phone and dialed zero.

"I'd like to place a collect call to Columbus, Ohio. The number is …" I told the operator.

About a minute later, I was talking with John Kady about his job offer.

"How about if I come down Wednesday afternoon of next week?" I asked.

That would give me plenty of time to do a lot of work. The first thing I did was leaf through the journalism history book I'd saved from college to refresh my memory on the founding of UPI. I also had to type up a résumé and gather a few stories I had written to update a portfolio.

Chapter 5

Sandi
Wednesday, November 8, 1967
Sandi Meets John

S omething deep inside told me I would have that Wednesday afternoon off. I toyed with the idea of asking for the afternoon off but hadn't come up with a logical excuse. I continued working as though nothing were planned. I didn't want to say anything about having a job offer for fear of someone spreading rumors. What would people think of me if I didn't do well on the interview, didn't like the offer, or something like that? Of course, if you tell one person, the rumor spreads rapidly and the story often changes. I didn't want that.

By the end of the week, reality set in. I had scheduled the interview without looking at a calendar. *How could you be so stupid?* I asked myself when I realized Wednesday was the day after an election. I would be putting in extra hours a couple of days before and on election night. I would be worn out by Wednesday afternoon and looking for the opportunity to get some sleep. And now I had a job interview.

"Take Wednesday afternoon off," the station manager, Robert Kincaid, told me. "You're doing a lot of work now, and you'll be in here much of Tuesday night. You've earned it."

His words were just what I had been hoping for, and I didn't even have to ask for it.

To me, election day seems to be a quiet news day. The major story is checking polling places and the elections board. Not many other things are happening. Perhaps everyone is waiting for the big news at night.

I turned twenty-one, the threshold for voting in those days, in college and had to vote in a general election, a special election, and a primary election by absentee ballot. The first election I could go to the polls, I was working in my hometown and living at home. I was up early. Mom made breakfast so we could vote, and then I would go to work. We were at the polling place when voting began, and I was the first in line. Ever since, I'm one of the first voters from my precinct. I find it a great way to start the day.

My regular routine of making phone calls, distributing the newssheet around town, and writing stories didn't produce much. I found a little color to add to my election story when I visited my polling place to see the turnout. Throughout the day I checked with the Board of Elections to get a handle on the voter turnout.

I recorded my Wednesday afternoon show Monday afternoon. I had a break Tuesday afternoon before the polls closed and was able to get a nap so I would be fresh for the long night ahead. Even though we were a small-wattage station and signed off at sundown, a few of us worked that night. I was at the station, monitoring reports from the AP wire for regional, state, and national results. Bill, the sales manager, was at the Board of Elections feeding me local results. Robert was in his office getting caught up on his work and pitching in wherever he was needed. Bob, the on-air disc jockey who also ran the control board, pulled music for the next day and left as we were getting busy.

Work slowed around midnight. Results were in and races had been decided. Now I had to write stories. Somewhere between writing stories for morning newscasts and getting ready to start a new day, I caught a couple of hours' sleep—on the engineer's worktable.

Sleep—or lack thereof—was beginning to catch up with me in the midmorning hours. Bill and I were sharing duties for an expanded 8:30 a.m. newscast. He usually read that newscast when I was on my trip through town, but this morning I would delay the rounds a few minutes and help with what was now a fifteen-minute newscast instead of the usual ten. I made it about halfway through before the giggles came. I put my stories on the table and ran out of the studio laughing, leaving Bill to do a few stories by himself. A drink of water, a few deep breaths, and I was back in the studio with him.

About noon I was exhausted.

"I'm outta here," I told the general manager and secretary around eleven thirty. "I'm done. Everything is in order for the rest of the day. Bob has everything he needs. We've been over it carefully. I'm going home to sleep."

"You earned it," the station manager said. "Good job last night."

I wondered how many of those long nights he had been through. He kept to himself that election night but occasionally slipped into my little room to see if I needed help. We both worked all night. When did he have time to sleep? I had been so involved in my work that I didn't pay attention to what he was doing.

When I arrived at my apartment, I didn't get that sleep. Instead I took a hot bath; put on a brown-and-white wool pleated skirt, a gold-colored sweater with white trim, and the jacket to match the skirt; and drove the nearly thirty miles to Columbus for the interview.

I was surprised at how easily I maneuvered my way through downtown Columbus and found the UPI office. Midafternoon didn't produce much traffic, and I was a little familiar with the downtown area. I had no idea what to expect when I walked back the long hallway of the building at 62 East Broad Street and opened the door.

An older gentleman casually dressed was typing on a teletype machine much like the one in my newsroom, only this one had a keyboard in front. Instead of keys hitting paper, the operator's typing punched holes in a strip of yellow tape that fed through a transmitter and produced capital letters on the paper in the machine.

At a desk within arm's reach was a young man wearing a shirt and tie. He was frantically typing and handing ivory-colored copy paper to the teletype operator. *Every journalist must use that paper*, I thought.

"I'm looking for John Kady," I said to the young man at the typewriter.

"Kady!" he yelled and continued his typing.

A slender man who looked a little older than I approached with his hand out. He didn't seem tall: he was perhaps about six inches taller than my five feet. He combed his hair in a floppy Princeton style made popular in the John Kennedy era and wore black-rimmed glasses.

"I'm John Kady, bureau manager for UPI in Ohio," he said.

I shook hands with him and introduced myself. I was about ten minutes early for my 3:00 p.m. interview. He was wearing a shirt with rolled-up sleeves and tie and stood at a configuration of four desks littered with newspapers and other sheets of paper, ashtrays filled with ashes and cigarette butts, and carryout cups with a bit of stale coffee in them and floating cigarette butts. Behind two of the desks on the dirty tile floor was a pile of newspapers, some still in mailing wrappers. I counted nine teletype machines lining the walls of that huge L-shaped room. Only a few of them were transmitting and making noise at that hour. I thought the clickety-clack of one machine in my little newsroom in Delaware was noisy. I couldn't imagine nine of them going at once.

John introduced me to the state editor, Ted Virostko, who handed me a story and asked me to write it in broadcast style. He wanted a three-sentence version and a three-paragraph one. The story he selected was the election of Carl Stokes as mayor of Cleveland, the first African American elected mayor of a major city.

John wheeled a metal typing table holding a yellow Royal typewriter, the vintage of my high school days, beside a teletype machine and pulled a wobbly desk chair with a cracked vinyl seat from a nearby table. I sat down and rolled the paper into the typewriter, trying not to seem rattled with one of the men in front of me and the other behind me. Teletype machines were on either side of me and several people were walking about. I didn't know it then, but it was change-of-shift time.

I was halfway through with the three-paragraph version of the story when Virostko reached over my shoulder, pulled the paper out of the typewriter, and said, "We're not going to have any problem with you. Here, fill out this application blank." I was still typing—only on the platen.

Thus began my wait. I kept in touch with UPI, especially following up on the death of the young woman. From the evidence found at the scene and extensive interviews with the family and friends, the police department soon closed the case, indicating the woman had taken her own life.

I didn't say anything about interviewing for a new job to people in Delaware, except for those whom I asked to serve as references. I wasn't sure when I was going to start at UPI or even if. All I knew was that I passed the writing test and filled out an application. That didn't necessarily guarantee a job.

I had been told I would replace Rick Van Sant, who was waiting for his call to active military duty. If I did replace him, I would have to relinquish my position when he returned. Where would that leave me? However, I did check with UPI about once a month or whenever I had a story to offer. I was assured I was at the top of the list.

The secrecy burst early in 1968 when Bill, our sales manager, the fire chief, and I were walking across the street together and the fire chief asked if I had heard anything about the new job.

Bill questioned me later, and I told him I had filled out an application and passed the writing test, but that was all. He told the station manager, and the station manager suggested I find my replacement. I started looking around for people interested in broadcasting. I even checked with a broadcast school in Columbus.

Then things started happening. The previous fall, the body of a man had been found in Delaware County, and a man from the Columbus suburb of Worthington had been charged with murder. The trial would begin in early March. The first of March is when the call came from UPI. When could I start?

"The best I can do is give a full two-weeks notice," I said.

That would make my first day Monday, March 18—the beginning of the second week of the murder trial, the first murder trial I had had an opportunity to cover. I had always wanted to cover a murder trial. And now that I had my chance, I also had to conduct interviews to find my replacement.

Fortunately I wasn't going to move. I was planning to stay in Delaware and drive back and forth to Columbus because I wasn't sure of the stability of the job or my financial situation.

I interviewed four people. One young man didn't even know how to put a sheet of paper in a typewriter, let alone write a story. He was from the broadcast school. I'm not sure what these students were being taught, but they carried more books than I had for all my journalism courses in college. I had said I was looking for someone to be a news director. When I spoke with the applicants, I advised them to write stories from the local newspaper in broadcast style. I don't think any of the four did, and I didn't see a résumé from any of them.

I didn't have much hope for the four people, but I chose one young lady whom I considered the best of the four. I invited her to shadow me for a couple of days so I could show her the routine I had developed. I also hoped she would learn from what I had done and would be able to expand on it as she developed her own routine.

I said my good-byes to many of my contacts in the downtown area on Friday and to my coworkers on Saturday. I was headed for the big city.

I would be a reporter for the wire service United Press International. I was going to work for a company known worldwide that had reporters all over the world. I hadn't been out of college three years.

I checked the few books I kept from college and found my journalism history book. I'd never discard that book: it held too many memories. I had read that book like a novel the first week of classes during winter quarter of my junior year at Kent State University. I listened to casual lectures, took notes, and crammed like mad the night before the two-hour final. It paid off. I aced the final, quite a coup since the professor didn't normally give As in his classes.

I started reading my journalism history again.

United Press International was a wire service that delivered stories and photos to newspapers and radio and TV stations around the world, but it wasn't the first. That distinction goes to the AP. UPI was sort of a Johnny-come-lately operation. The two went head-to-head. I was going to bat in a new ballpark.

Chapter 6

Sandi

1968

How I Got Where I Am Today

As a child, I gave much thought to what I was going to be when I grew up. My father had always stressed that I was going to college and that I should set myself up in a career so that if I found myself in a position of supporting a family, I could. I realize now that that was kind of forward thinking in the 1950s for a girl who grew up in north central Ohio in a rural area.

I toyed with a few occupations or careers. I often played librarian, setting my books up on a table in our tent in the backyard and checking one out and going somewhere to read. Also frequently crossing my mind was an airline stewardess—never mind that I had never been in an airplane. Somewhere along the way I learned about a height requirement. I was on the small side. What could I expect from a father who was five-foot-four or so and a mother at five-foot-two? I decided I would never make it to the minimum height. Today I barely measure five feet, and I still can't reach the overhead compartments. I have to use the book I'm reading to turn on the light over my seat.

I was twelve years old in the spring of 1956. My parents were going to take my younger brother to the barbershop in the neighboring county one evening. I didn't want to go.

"I can stay by myself," I started the plea to stay home.

After laying the ground rules, my parents felt they could trust me. I had to stay in the house or on the porch. I had to do my homework.

"I will," I pledged.

Shortly after my parents pulled out of the driveway, I went into their bedroom, got their radio, plugged it into an extension cord, and carried the radio to the front porch. I thought I would get music on the radio. I wasn't going to change the station because I didn't want them to know I had borrowed the radio. I was afraid that if I changed the station, I wouldn't be able to get their station back.

Instead of music, WJR in Detroit was broadcasting a baseball game. The Tigers beat the Washington Senators that night. The next day I had something to talk about with the boys in my class. I didn't realize the Tigers were mired in the bottom third of the American League and had been and would be for years.

I continued to listen to the Tigers on WJR on my little ivory-colored radio that had an antenna wired to an alligator clip that I attached to the bedsprings. Within days, I decided what I wanted to do with my life.

"I want to be a baseball announcer," I said to my father one evening after he had returned from a trip where he had been hauling burial vaults to far-off cities.

"If you want to be a baseball announcer, you have to learn journalism," was his advice.

I knew he would help me. When my third-grade teacher complained about my poor penmanship, I said, "I'm not worried. Daddy will get me a typewriter."

Two summers later when my grandfather passed away, Daddy brought home Grandmother's black Underwood standard typewriter, borrowed a typing manual from the nearby school, and let me learn by myself. When my grandmother decided she wanted the typewriter back, Daddy bought a portable Smith Corona, a little brown and green typewriter that went through life with me until computers came on the scene.

I didn't give journalism another thought, but I did think about being a baseball announcer. My main reason? I could pronounce the players' names. I was a little young to think about pursuing a career. I was only in the seventh grade and not yet a teenager.

A few weeks after school started in the fall, life began to change. We lived around the corner from the school, and the principal's family lived on the other side of the school. The principal's wife was the area correspondent to the local paper, the *Bucyrus Telegraph-Forum*. One day she talked with my parents and me about taking over her job.

She said I was closer to the school and church than she was and wanted to know if I would like to do it.

"You can try it, and if you don't like it, you don't have to keep it," my father said.

My mother took me into town to the newspaper office, where I had an interview with "Doc" Kirby, the person in charge of the area correspondents. He gave me a little handbook of how to write newspaper stories. I still have that handbook.

I was now a reporter. Mom drove me around the neighborhood so I could get reports of church meetings and events. I wrote the neighbor girl's engagement announcement and later her wedding story. I wrote about meetings at the school and activities at the church next door. Every time I had a story to submit, Mom drove me into town some five miles away to drop my story in the correspondents' basket. Every month I received a check in the mail.

My reputation grew. My freshman year in high school, I was elected news reporter for Future Homemakers of America. That meant I had to take home economics. I struggled through canning peaches and tomatoes, which I had helped my mother do a few weeks earlier. I learned to fix different types of eggs, while at home I was making chili and potato salad for the restaurant my parents had bought just a few weeks earlier.

I didn't take home economics my sophomore year because it fell at the same time as Latin class, and I had to have a foreign language to go to college. By this time I was serious about my career choice. I was in a small school system, with only about three hundred people from first grade through twelfth.

My senior year in high school was a turning point for me. My father had passed away the last day of my junior year, and I seemed on my own. Mother and I weren't that close. I made a lot of decisions about the restaurant, handled the bookwork, and wrote checks for both the restaurant and home.

When it came time to choose a college, I selected Kent State after doing my own research. Dad had wanted me to go to Ohio State, but I said it was too big. Mom had wanted me to go to Ohio University and live with her sister. No way! The decision was my own, as was my choice of a career. I had no opposition from Mom. She was living her own life, and remarried a few months after I left for college.

I started college in January 1962, the day after I resigned as area correspondent to the local newspaper, a position I had held for five years. I started one quarter later than others with whom I graduated. The person I had sent my college application to was on vacation, but forwarded it to the proper person when he returned. That was too late for fall-quarter admission. One summer of classes and my internship a second summer allowed me to complete my four years in three and a half.

My first year in college, I concentrated on getting some required courses out of the way. I didn't take any journalism classes until my sophomore year. I was the only one in the first-year writing class who had had any newspaper experience. I also started working at the *Daily Kent Stater*, the daily campus newspaper. In my junior and senior years, I did proofreading on the yearbook, the *Chestnut Burr*.

The summer between my junior and senior years, I had to do an internship. That's like student teaching, but we journalism students chose to do it in summer because not only did we get nine credit hours, but we also were paid.

I tried to get a job around Kent but had no luck. As spring quarter came to an end, I still didn't have an internship. Radio stations didn't want to hire summer help, train them, and lose them. If I didn't have experience, how could I get a job?

Back in my small hometown of Bucyrus, radio station WBCO was new to the community. The studios were in an old home built during the Civil War. The station had been on the air only a few months by the time I needed the internship. The first day I was home, I went to the radio station at eight in the morning and sat on the porch waiting for Tom Moore, the general manager, to arrive.

"Tom, you have an opening and I need an internship," I begged of him.

Maybe he felt sorry for me, or maybe he wanted the help. He and I sat and talked. He took down all my information, including my advisor's name and phone numbers at Kent.

A couple of days later, Tom called. I had the job. I would be working an 8:00 a.m. to 5:00 p.m. shift Monday through Friday and 8:00 a.m. to 12:00 noon on Saturday. I would write commercial copy, public service announcements, and some news. I accompanied the salesmen on sales calls to advertisers. I worked with Tom's wife, LaVonne, who had a women's show. I watched the disc jockeys on the control board. I learned how to record the reports from the hospitals and livestock yards. I even had the opportunity to cover city council and school board meetings at night.

Most of all, I enjoyed going with the sports reporter, Doyle Weaver, to Little League games. I was doing a little broadcast work and keeping score.

I went back to Kent that fall with the advice from Tom at WBCO that "if we have an opening here when you graduate, you have a job."

One of my professors, who had read my weekly reports that summer, let me lead the class when we were studying coverage of city council and school boards.

That spring, a few weeks before graduation, I stopped at WBCO to chat with Tom.

"When do you graduate?" he asked.

"June 15," I said.

"I'll expect you at 8:00 a.m. on June 17," he said, extending his hand.

I was the last person in my journalism class to get an internship and the only one who had a job the Monday after graduation.

I worked at WBCO 44 hours a week, making a little more than I had the summer before when I was classified a student learner. A little more than fifteen months after I started as a full-time employee, I heard about a woman working at a station in Delaware. I had to go through Delaware one day on my way to a Columbus hospital to visit a relative of my stepfather. I stopped at my aunt's house in Delaware and called this woman; she said she would talk with me. However, when I went to see her, she had changed her mind. Instead, I spoke with the general manager and the executive vice president, who was visiting from Kentucky, where WDLR had a sister station.

About a week later, I realized that the conversation with those two gentlemen was a job offer. As we had talked about the type of news coverage we were doing at WBCO, one of them asked, "Do you have a twin sister as good on news as you are?"

I wasn't even on the news staff; I was the production director, but that didn't matter.

This conversation haunted me. I decided to call and talk to them again. I called the general manager and made an appointment for the following Saturday afternoon. It was a strange time for an interview, but the best I could manage. I was going to Columbus that weekend, Labor Day weekend, for a theatrical production the Bucyrus Little Theater was staging at the Ohio State Fair. I was spending the weekend with friends in Columbus.

I put on a lavender-and-white dress and white heels, put white gloves in my purse, and carried a small portfolio in a notebook. I headed for Columbus, with a stop in Delaware.

When I arrived at the station, the young man working the control board called the station manager, who was at home mowing his lawn. He came in, dressed in Madras shorts and grass-stained tennis shoes, wiped his hands on his shorts, and extended his hand, saying, "When do you want to start?"

We settled on two weeks from Monday.

When I returned home Labor Day afternoon, I told my mom and stepdad of my new job and called my boss, Tom, to offer my resignation.

"He'll offer you more money to stay," my stepdad Bill maintained, not understanding that I had an opportunity to advance in my career and to use my college education in a different area.

Tom didn't offer a pay raise, only his hand and a send-off of "Good luck!"

Two weeks later, I had an apartment in Delaware and a few items for the kitchen to go with the bedroom suite I'd had since the eighth grade. I was excited. I was on my own. The day I started at WDLR was the second day of the Delaware County Fair, three days before the Little Brown Jug harness horse race, and the day before classes began at Ohio Wesleyan University. I was in a town where I knew four people: my mother's sister and her husband, and her brother and his wife.

I walked into the studio that morning and got the attention of the guy on the control board. I introduced myself and asked where the news director was so I could get my assignments.

"Ma'am, you are the news director," he informed me.

Chapter 7

John
1968
How I Got Where I Am Today

I'm the oldest of six boys in the Kady family. Dad was a principal in a public school. Although we are Catholic, all of us boys went to the public school. Some people might think that was strange.

"What would the people think if you went to a Catholic school?" Dad would say. "If a public school is good enough for me to work in, it's good enough for you to get your education."

We followed him to school, and he expected us to go to college afterward. Five of us did.

When I graduated from Union High School in Benwood, West Virginia, in May 1951, it didn't look as though I would make it to college. I didn't know what I wanted to be when I grew up. I had thought of journalism after watching some Jimmy Cagney and Humphrey Bogart movies, but I didn't pursue it. Besides, I didn't have a foreign language from high school to get into college.

I knew foreign languages all right but couldn't count them as required courses in school. Benwood is in the northern panhandle of West Virginia, about three miles from Wheeling. Coal mining was the main industry, and many of those miners came from other areas of the world. We had Serbs, Croats, Hungarians, and Irish families in the area. With all their children in school, it seemed that English was a foreign language.

In my school days, Latin was the only foreign language offered, and I never considered taking it. Besides, I played football and it wouldn't be cool. Anyway, I couldn't find time to fit it into my schedule. By the time I was a junior, I didn't want to be with the freshmen who were taking the class.

After graduation, while many of my classmates were preparing to go to college, I was heading east. A cousin had told me about a position as clerk-typist in the Pentagon, where he worked. I packed up my few belongings and moved in with my grandmother in Alexandria, Virginia, and went to work at the Pentagon for the Department of the Army. I was typing reports sent from all the military bases and the Signal Corps. There I was, seventeen years old, and had top secret clearance.

I was there for nine months, quitting a few weeks before I enlisted in the air force for four years. Two of those years were spent on Okinawa, where I was assigned to the air police and worked with dogs. Our group patrolled the base perimeter with German shepherds to stop the Okinawans from sneaking on base and stealing anything they could get their hands on. My final two years were spent at bases in the United States, with the exception of a short stint in England, where I guarded airplanes that were a part of the Strategic Air Command.

When I was discharged in January 1956, I decided to use my $21 a month from the GI Bill to go to college. I enrolled in West Virginia University in February at the start of the second semester, majoring in business administration.

Flunking an accounting course sent me looking for a new major. Remembering an early idea of wanting to be a journalist, I enrolled in the journalism school.

I still needed that foreign language. Even though I was now a college student, I knew I had to enroll in a language class. I chose Russian, and for two years worked hard at that strange language. I had visions of becoming a foreign correspondent and thought Russian would help me. After all, this was the beginning of the space age and Russia had launched Sputnik. The little Japanese I learned on Okinawa was limited and didn't meet any requirements.

To get some experience in journalism, I joined the staff of the daily student newspaper, the *Athenaeum*. I served as sports editor, copy editor, proofreader, and chief photographer. I was paid $50 a semester for each of these jobs. That money and the $21 from the GI Bill helped out tremendously because by my junior year, I was supporting my wife, Joyce, and infant daughter, Jennifer.

With graduation approaching in the spring of 1959, I had to find a job. Thank heaven for the editor of the Morgantown newspaper, who offered me a position as sportswriter, but that fell through when the fellow I was to replace decided to stay.

"I can put in a good word for you with both Associated Press and United Press International," he said. The editor had gotten to know us WVU students since our daily newspaper was published at his printing press and he read that paper every day.

"I'll go with UPI," I offered.

"Any reason?" the editor asked.

"I got to know the UPI wire because it was in the *Athenaeum*," I said.

Thus began a career with the wire service. It lasted nearly thirty-five years and put me in touch with major events, well-known individuals, and some terrific workers. I have a close friendship today with many people who worked for me and with me over the years.

My first job was in the UPI office in Charleston, West Virginia. I'll never forget my first assignment.

"This guy is running in West Virginia," the state editor told me. "You go with him. Call me with everything he says and does."

In the field with other reporters I thought, *What am I doing?* "This guy" I was told to follow was John F. Kennedy, and he was running a Democratic presidential primary campaign in the West Virginia coal mining area. What was a Catholic doing in this strong Protestant region? West Virginia had only eight electoral votes, not enough to be considered a swing state.

That same John F. Kennedy, the young Massachusetts senator with a strong, hard-to-understand New England accent, was taking on a veteran politician, Minnesota Senator Hubert H. Humphrey.

That day the media folks jumped in press cars to follow Kennedy. I hopped in a car. I was in the back seat between veteran reporters Bob Considine of Hearst Newspapers and David Brinkley from NBC News.

I was in awe. I had to show that I could hold my ground with the best of them, but I knew I could learn from them. I listened to them as much as I listened to the candidates.

When I wasn't covering the political scene, I was covering West Virginia University sports and even the legislature. Versatility—being able to write a variety of stories—is an asset at a wire service. Throughout my career I found a few colleagues who could do it without grumbling. Some people want to specialize in one area and resent it when they are asked to do something else.

In September 1963, I was transferred to Baltimore, where I was to be the Baltimore bureau manager as well as Maryland state editor. I packed up Joyce and two daughters, Jennifer and Gretchen, and moved to the East Coast.

The Baltimore bureau had three employees. I was the fourth one. This wasn't West Virginia by any means. West Virginia's main industry was coal mining. In Maryland the fishing industry was big. Where West Virginia was highly rural outside of Charleston and other larger cities such as Wheeling, Beckley, and Huntington, the Baltimore area was highly urban, and not far from Washington, DC.

Kennedy was elected president in 1960 and took office in January 1961. One big issue under discussion in Congress was civil rights. It was also being fought in the streets.

In nearby North Carolina, Negroes—as they were called then—staged sit-ins at the lunch counters at Woolworth stores to strengthen their demand to eat alongside whites. In Baltimore, they staged protests. Many Negroes were calling for desegregation—a full nine years after *Brown v. Board of Education*, which eventually resulted in desegregating schools in Little Rock, Arkansas, and subsequently the calling out of the National Guard.

Baltimore's fights went to the streets, and I went right into the groups. I got to know the demonstrators as I interviewed them for stories.

What made the situation more tense were the visits of Stokely Carmichael and Alabama Governor George Wallace at the same time. Carmichael was a well-known civil rights leader. In 1966, the activist would make the phrase "Black Power" popular—calling on blacks to unite and build a sense of community. Wallace was one who put up resistance to the civil rights movement.

In time, the rioting calmed, and I turned to sports, covering the Baltimore Colts of the National Football League and the Baltimore Bullets of the National Basketball Association and writing feature stories on the Baltimore Orioles.

After two years in Baltimore, UPI asked me to take over as bureau manager in Louisville, Kentucky. Again Joyce and the girls, little more than toddlers, moved with me.

Back to the coalfields, I thought, but the big story I covered was Muhammad Ali. He had started his boxing career as Cassius Clay and changed his name when he converted to the Muslim faith. Then came the military draft, which he was fighting. He wanted to be declared a conscientious objector, claiming he was a pacifist.

He was facing the possibility of being sent to Vietnam as a stretcher bearer, and he didn't want to go to the combat zone. He didn't think his chances of survival would be very high. His attorney was trying to get the judge to declare as unconstitutional the provision that allowed conscientious objectors to be sent to combat zones as stretcher bearers.

I scored a few scoops on this story because I had made friends with his mother and she let me know when he was coming to town. I would be at the airport when he arrived to interview him before any other reporters did.

After two years in Louisville, I got a call to go to Columbus, Ohio, as bureau manager.

Another move. It was beginning to wear on Joyce and the two girls.

"John, you have to get an assignment where you can settle down," she said. "The girls are starting school, and I don't want to uproot them every other year."

As much as I loved my work, the challenges, the people I covered, and seeing journalists develop into better writers, I knew Joyce was right. I had responsibilities. My father had had a stable position and our family didn't move around, but I was a member of a different generation and I held a different job.

I arrived in Ohio in January 1967. Although Ohio borders West Virginia and Kentucky, things are different. Legislatures in West Virginia and Kentucky met for two or three months. In Ohio, the legislature met nearly all year.

I quickly learned I couldn't assign one of the staff members to the Statehouse for three or four months as was done in neighboring states. UPI in Ohio had a Statehouse bureau, with a staff of one and sometimes two.

Coal was mined in Ohio, but it wasn't as big an industry as it was in West Virginia or Kentucky. Agriculture was the number one industry. The auto industry was growing, and steel mills in northern Ohio were producing. Ohio State University, up the street from the UPI office, had the nation's largest enrollment, and a top football team drew one of the largest crowds in the nation every home game. In the summer, the governor, Jim Rhodes, proclaimed the Ohio State Fair the greatest in the nation. When he wasn't expounding on "a diploma in one hand, a job in the other," he was traveling the country and the world seeking more industry for a state he loved dearly.

Columbus wasn't a UPI office where the state editor or bureau manager, titles I held simultaneously elsewhere, had a regular beat. As bureau manager, I worked the main desk during the week. That meant I was writing stories every day, whether they were rewrites from newspapers, stories that our stable of stringers called in, stories developed from news releases, or stories dictated from the happenings on the street.

I had the luxury of having a broadcast writer on two shifts a day six days a week, a sportswriter that I lobbied to make into a full-time position, and often a person on rewrite. Nearly all of them could write any kind of story that confronted them. I made out the schedules. I made a point of learning what my staff could do and put them to work in areas where they excelled.

As state editor, I oversaw work in the four offices in Ohio—Cleveland and Cincinnati as well as Columbus and the Statehouse—and worked closely with our clients, both newspaper and broadcast.

Toward the end of my career, I took on an assignment on the other side of the desk—that of selling our service to newspapers and broadcasters.

Book 2

1968–1989

Chapter 8

John
January 1967
Welcome to Ohio

I welcomed the new year of 1967 by moving to Columbus, Ohio, and taking over as bureau manager. I was anxious to continue learning as I performed a job I knew I could do.

Much of my job was working the day news desk. I maintained a five-day-a-week routine, as did everyone on my staff, but when I made out the schedule, I had to have people working around the clock, seven days a week. That meant some people had to work different shifts during the week, and some had days off in the middle of the week.

I had a broadcast writer on two shifts Monday through Saturday, and the state editor worked alongside the teletype operator filing the newspaper wire Monday through Friday. Dayside was busier, and I often had a rewrite person who could be sent out to cover events and write the stories as well as work in the office with me. The night shift that began at 3:00 p.m. had only two people—the night desk person also filed copy for the morning newspapers. At that time, UPI had few Ohio papers publishing in the mornings.

Newspapers that arrive on the doorstep in the morning are AM papers and are put together in the evenings and late at night. Those that are available around noontime and early afternoon are PM papers and are put together in the early and midmornings.

I never gave it a second thought that years later most newspapers would be publishing as AMers.

The third shift, known as the overnight, began at 10:30 p.m. and was a one-person operation on news, working with one teletype operator. The operator's shift was over in the middle of the night, leaving the overnight person alone for about an hour and a half until the daytime operators arrived around five o'clock.

I had to get used to the three shifts. This was the first time I had ever worked in a UPI bureau that operated around the clock. I had a young staff. Only two were older than my thirty-four years: Bob Grimm was nearing two decades on working both sports and news, while Mason Blosser had about that many years on the night news desk.

My shift started at 6:00 a.m. The first thing I did was read our report to see what stories we were carrying for that cycle. Then I checked the local newspaper to see if it had any story we didn't.

The broadcast editor, who also arrived at 6:00 a.m., and I took turns answering phones and writing stories that came from calls from our stringers. By the time the mail arrived, so did the state editor, who would mark up copy for the newspaper wire.

Copy came over the wires in all capital letters. If the story was on the national or A wire, it would run on the newspaper wire. If it came from a lesser wire and had to be punched by an operator, the person filing the newspaper wire would have to mark up the copy—three lines under letters that should be capitalized, other copyediting marks signifying centered and boldfaced bylines, and any other editing notations as needed.

Before I took a lunch break, I had written the sked, or budget as some papers called it—the list of stories that would be running for the next cycle. After lunch I would do the necessary paperwork, such as making out schedules and compiling stringer payment lists.

It was a quiet start. I was able to get Joyce and the girls settled in what I was hoping would be an assignment that lasted more than two years, but I knew that quietness would not last.

It was an odd-numbered year and the start of a two-year session for the Ohio Legislature. James Rhodes was inaugurated to start his second four-year term. The big item of business for the legislature was developing a budget that would take effect in July. Work to get a budget in place would take nearly six months.

Dick Lightner was our Statehouse bureau manager and could handle quite a bit of the work himself, but when activity heated up, I called on Dick Wheeler, a young energetic reporter, as my go-to guy to assist him. The two could work efficiently and effectively together. If Wheeler wasn't helping with Statehouse coverage, he was working the third shift.

I had a quiet couple of months until the first Sunday evening of March.

"John. Mason Blosser here." I heard the voice of my Sunday night desk man. "A Lake Central airliner went down in northwest Ohio. Everyone is feared dead."

I knew I would have to send a reporter and a photographer to the scene, but it would take nearly two hours for the reporter and photographer to get from Columbus to Wyandot County, about seventy-five miles away. In the meantime, we would have to rely on information for a story from our closest clients as well as what was available from the airline and investigators.

The plane was carrying thirty-eight people and had gone down in a field in rural northwest Ohio. Everyone died.

The crash was the lead story for a couple of days; then the lengthy investigation by the National Transportation Safety Board began. It would be several months, maybe a year, before we learned the cause of the crash. The NTSB ruled that one of the engines failed and the propeller speeded up. The blades broke off and one went through the fuselage.

Meanwhile, I was learning about Ohio—its geography, history, politics, who and what made the state run. I was also getting to know our clients, both newspaper and broadcast.

Springtime brought a primary election, with winners advancing to the November ballot. Students at Oberlin College in northeast Ohio protested actions surrounding involvement in the Vietnam War. Coverage of those activities was handled through the Cleveland bureau.

The Cincinnati Reds and Cleveland Indians were no threat for the World Series, even though the Reds introduced a young catcher by the name of Johnny Bench in late August.

About the same time, we covered a skydiving tragedy over Lake Erie. Seventeen skydivers jumped out of a plane thinking they were over land, but in reality, the plane was over Lake Erie. Two skydivers were rescued and fifteen were lost. All but one body was recovered. I sent a young reporter to Cleveland to start the coverage after the Sunday tragedy, and Cleveland reporters took over the next day.

The general election that November was a mayoral election. Cleveland voters elected Carl Stokes their first African American mayor and the first African American to lead a major city.

The day after an election is always a busy day. Our clients and stringers called in throughout the day with reports of races in their areas. I even took time that afternoon to interview a young broadcast reporter to whom I had offered a job.

One thing that we in the news business do in early December is sort through the events of the previous eleven months and pick our top ten stories. The plane crash, student unrest and demonstrations, the death of the skydivers all mingled with political news, weather, sports, and the economy.

The list was compiled and the story written, just waiting to be sent out to our clients.

And then it all changed.

A Friday night in mid-December I got a phone call at home—a bridge over the Ohio River near Gallipolis had collapsed into the river during evening rush hour. It was also Christmas shopping season and a high school basketball night, which meant a lot of people out on the roads.

I called on Wheeler to go to the disaster site.

The bridge cracked at 5:00 p.m. Thirty-one of the thirty-seven vehicles on the bridge fell with the bridge, twenty-four of them into the icy waters and the others onto the Ohio shore. Forty-six people died, and nine were injured.

I was beginning to look forward to 1968.

Chapter 9

Sandi
March 18, 1968
My UPI Career Begins

I was up early the morning of Monday, March 18, 1968—the middle of the night by some people's standards—taking care to dress for a new job in the big city. Since it was my first day to work in Columbus, I didn't know much about traffic. I was able to ride the thirty miles with a friend so I could become accustomed to traffic and learn where to park. Normally the day shift at UPI began at 6:00 a.m., but this first week, for training, my shift was 9:00 a.m. to 6:00 p.m., with an hour for lunch. That coincided with my friend's work shift.

As I entered the UPI offices, I found the layout the same as it was a few months ago—two desks sitting back-to-back with two others abutting at one end. Those who worked at the desks that sat back-to-back had typewriters on metal typing tables, similar to the one my father bought when I was in elementary school.

John sat at one desk, while Jeff on broadcast sat at the desk facing him. I was shown to one on the end. It was an old wooden desk with a flat lid that could be dropped down in back to elevate a typewriter. I don't think that typewriter had been hidden for many years, and it would never be hidden in the years I spent in that room.

The typewriters were yellow and gray Royals, about as old as the ones I had used in high school in the late 1950s and early sixties. Those had been used for several years. At least they were easy to use, not like the black square Underwood from my grandmother that I learned on when I was eleven years old.

"Go down to the front door and get the mailbag," John told me.

I walked back down the hallway to get the big canvas bag with a UPI tag on it that the postal carrier left. Several bags were piled in the corner for the occupants in the building and I had to find ours. Back down the long hallway I went, dragging our mailbag behind me.

"Go through the mail," John advised me.

I unclasped the snap on the bag and dumped the contents onto the floor. Newspapers slid out, and a bundle of envelopes secured by a rubber band. The bundle was the size of a brick. I sorted the mail to be distributed to the news desk and the sports desk and put the two piles on John's desk. He would go through the mail, pulling out releases that sounded promising for turning into stories. The sports editor did the same with his pile.

My first writing task was to work with the stories that had been written for the newspapers and write them for broadcast. Short items were WIBs—short for World in Brief—and the longer items were roundup items. The WIBs would be used in radio stations for reporters' five-minute newscasts every hour. Television stations could use the roundup items for newscasts at noon, 6:00 p.m. and 11:00 p.m.

As I started writing, Ted Virostko stopped by to see how I was doing. He even complimented me on one of my three-sentence WIBs. The story was about a small plane that crashed in Medina County and the pilot escaped injury. The crash had happened Sunday, March 17, and I used an old cliché: "The luck of the Irish was with the pilot of a small plane."

"That's good, ma'am," he said, patting my shoulder. He always called me ma'am.

I knew from my experience at the radio stations to put the stories in the order of importance. That story about the plane crash from the day before, where no one was seriously injured, would be written once and placed toward the bottom of the items. Breaking and developing stories would go at the top and be rewritten every hour.

I think I wrote more copy that day than Jeff, who was assigned to the broadcast desk. It helped me learn the operation. These stories I was writing were sent to radio and TV stations and read by newscasters, as I had done for the past eighteen months at WDLR Radio.

The packages I helped write were transmitted every hour on the half hour, all day long, at the time a station would be putting together a newscast. Sports and weather forecasts and market reports were sent when received. Sports is always big news. Ohio is an agricultural state and that was the number one industry, so the farm market reports were important.

State bureaus would transmit their copy for twenty minutes beginning on the half hour. The remaining part of the hour was dedicated to national news transmitted from the national broadcast desk in Chicago. If we had a breaking story when national was transmitting, we could break in and transmit our bulletin, then return the wire to the national desk.

UPI and the Associated Press were the two wire services going head-to-head in the news business, doing the same type of work from different locations and transmitting news to their clients. Some newspapers and radio and TV stations at that time carried both services, and the business became competitive. Who had it first? Who wrote it better? Whose story would be used in those two-service papers? We each wanted to win.

In Ohio at that time were several newspapers that subscribed to both UPI and AP. Every day we would get a call from one of those papers, the *Dayton Daily News*, with the list of stories in its front section and whether it was the UPI or the AP version.

I soon learned how to type up the logs—a listing of what stories were used in those papers. If the story were a UPI one, we put down the numeral 1; if AP, we put down 2. It looked like this: Undated Weather 1, HX explosion 2. Undated meant it didn't have a dateline. The word weather was the slug or what the story was about. The HX in the second listing showed the explosion story was from Chicago.

By the middle of the afternoon, someone in New York (NX) had compiled the logs sent from throughout the country and transmitted that tabulation to each bureau. We could tell how we were doing against our competition in major stories. We won some; we lost some.

Each bureau had a two-letter designation. We were CZ. Only St. Louis had a one-letter designation—X. Honolulu for years was known as 99. When computers arrived, 99 became HONO. We used the bureau call letters to send messages on the message wire, kind of like e-mail today, and signed them with our last name and bureau. I was Gould/CZ.

The AP may have pioneered a broadcast wire, but it was UPI that packaged it according to how radio stations, and later TV, could use it. When I worked at WDLR with AP copy, I had individual stories, but at UPI we put the stories into packages. It looked neater and was easy to handle on the other end. WBCO in Bucyrus had been a UPI subscriber, and I remembered the packaged items from the little bit I had worked with them.

My first week I worked Monday, Wednesday, Thursday, Friday, and Saturday, with Sunday and Tuesday off. Tuesday, for want of something to do, I went back to the Delaware County courtroom for the first-degree murder trial I had covered the previous week. I had always wanted to cover a murder trial and now that I had the opportunity, I couldn't continue covering it. Sitting in the courtroom as a spectator that day, I couldn't believe the following I had in Delaware.

"Won't you quit that job and come back to us?" I heard many times that day.

The defendant was convicted in the third week of the trial and sentenced to life in prison. Although I wasn't in the courtroom for the conclusion, I followed the trial through the Columbus newspapers and after the sentencing, was able to write a few paragraphs.

I couldn't quit my new job. I was moving up. I was able to put my college education to use in a different way. I was writing news stories that were being used by other people, and after only one day on the new job, I could see many opportunities ahead of me. I couldn't come back to a small radio station.

When I returned to work Wednesday, I was assigned to the broadcast desk by myself. Jeff had been working the dayside broadcast desk, but he was now assigned to nightside.

Driving home that day, I was listening to a station that had the UPI service and I heard stories I had written. I was surprised to hear my stories read the way I had written them. What a feeling of pride! My heart beat harder. I gripped the wheel tighter, and I read along with the newscaster. Hearing my work on the air also brought me into reality. Could I understand what I had written? It could help me improve my work.

I also had the opportunity to write stories for newspapers, and I worked from these stories to rewrite them into broadcast style. I was learning by doing. I loved the job, the work, and the people.

Saturday, even though it was a weekend and not much was happening, I still put on a skirt and blouse and heels. It was the late sixties and women were not wearing slacks to the office, or even dressing down on nights and weekends. John had had a day off in the middle of the week, and he and I were working together. It was quieter on Saturday than it had been during the week. Rarely did anyone walk in with a news release. City, county, and state offices were closed on weekends.

At a quiet time in the middle of the shift, John sat at the desk across from me, folded his hands in prayer, and said, "Airplane flying over Ohio, please fall out of the sky."

"Why are you doing that?" I asked.

"We need a story," he said.

A coworker praying for a disaster to happen? What had I gotten myself into?

Chapter 10

Sandi

Spring 1968
Learning the Ropes

The 1960s were a pivotal period in history. The baby boomers were coming of age. I was a little ahead of that group, having been born during World War II. After that war, servicemen and their families had helped create the suburbs and a new lifestyle.

By the time I was finishing college in 1965, the baby boomers were expressing themselves. They chose to do it in various ways. At some colleges, some students waged their protests by sit-ins. At Kent State, we had a few demonstrations. Students carried placards calling for students' rights, freedom of speech, and freedom of assembly. In the latter part of my senior year, I remember a half dozen or so students in jeans and colorful T-shirts who carried placards stating their demands and walked in circles in front of the administration building. One fellow represented the Congress of Racial Equality (CORE) and visited the office of the student newspaper—*Daily Kent Stater*—almost weekly. A young woman who marched with him wore what I considered mismatched clothes—a plaid skirt that came between her knees and ankles and a flowered blouse—and had a little bounce in her step. More students watched these demonstrations than participated.

After I graduated, the demonstrations grew in size and number and moved into other areas, including the streets. Violence was becoming more commonplace with them.

I had read articles in newspapers and from the newswires of such actions, but I now found myself in a different position—that of a reporter in a bigger arena than my college campus or a small town. I was writing stories and sending them to the newspapers and radio and TV stations throughout Ohio, the nation, and sometimes the world.

I had worked at UPI for three weeks when that all clicked and I was pressed into all kinds of writing.

Because I wasn't working at the radio station in Delaware, I felt I could become involved in community activities. I accepted the challenge of helping the March of Dimes in a fund-raising drive. My assignment was to visit the city's two bowling alleys and hand out information about a special promotion among bowlers and collect donations. It was while I was picking up those donations the evening of April 4, 1968, that I learned of the assassination of Martin Luther King Jr. in Memphis, Tennessee.

I stood in stunned silence in front of the TV at the bowling alley. Another assassination. I thought back five years to the killing of President Kennedy. *Why would anyone do such an act?*

The next morning at the office, I wrote broadcast items for a different type of story—a sidebar. This is an item on the same topic of the main story, but it contains a different type of information. In this case, the main story was the assassination; whereas this sidebar contained comments from Ohio people who knew Martin Luther King Jr., had worked with him, or were leaders in the African American community. Among the first to offer comment was Cleveland Mayor Carl Stokes. Statements also came from the governor, Ohio's two senators, and African American leaders. Since the shooting occurred while King was rallying support for the garbage collectors' strike in Memphis, comment came from the union locals of public employees.

Many times the comments were called in to the news desk by a public information officer or delivered to the office in a news release. Sometimes the statements went to our Statehouse bureau and the person there would walk across the street with it. If we felt we needed a comment from a specific person, we would call to see if it was available.

I tried not to let my feelings slip into my writing. That was part of my training—learning to write without bias. "Tell it straight" is what I was taught, and this was a good example of that training. The Rev. Dr. King was doing what he thought he had to do. I didn't think it should result in violence. I couldn't let that attitude creep into my writing.

A story of this nature gets top billing for a day since it didn't happen in Ohio. By the next day, it was back to normal, or as normal as it could be. For a few more weeks, at least.

Then came the middle of May. Student unrest at Ohio University started the week's news, followed by a fatal fire at the Ohio State University in the middle of the week and flooding in southeastern Ohio to end the week. Three major stories in five days. All were sent to our New York office to send out on the national wire. The UPI editors' conference was that weekend. Editors of our client newspapers gathered with UPI leaders to discuss how we could better meet their needs. To compound things, one person in the office had an eye infection, and another person had just been let go. Each shift had to be covered. I was asked to work six days that week, and they were twelve-hour shifts.

Even though I was working on the broadcast desk, I helped out on reporting and writing. Many stories we were working on were happening outside of Columbus, so in between writing my broadcast reports, I would make phone calls to a law enforcement officer, a hospital, or a municipal official. Sometimes I'd pass my notes to the person writing the main story; at other times I would write the story.

I quickly learned what makes a national story and that I had to write it so that a paper in another state would want to use it. In college, we often heard the phrase about "writing for the Kansas City milkman." I also learned at UPI that there was "a deadline every minute." It seemed we were always on a deadline, especially on the broadcast desk.

Student unrest was in its infancy in the mid to late sixties. That always drew attention. Weather-related stories were forwarded because they were used in the daily weather story. A fire that killed one person didn't usually garner more than two or three paragraphs for local use, but in this case, it was a fire in one of the towers used for a student residence hall on a large and prominent college campus. That was different, unusual, and therefore, newsworthy.

Chapter 11

John
Spring 1968
My Version of the Fire

Wednesday morning started off quietly for a change. I lit a Lucky Strike cigarette and picked up the file of stories that had already been transmitted to clients. I needed to familiarize myself with what was going on and what follow-ups we had to do.

The phone rang. I answered it. On the other end was a reporter from a radio station down the street: WCOL. The reporter told me a student had died in a fire in one of the towers at OSU.

Ohio State had recently completed two twelve-story towers for use as student residence halls. One was for male students, the other for female. Each suite housed four to six students. In the suite where the fire started, the women were overcome with smoke and one died.

Sandi and I hopped on the phones, calling the Columbus Fire Department because the university didn't have a fire department. We also put in calls to the Ohio State communications office seeking information and comment.

I wrote the story and had it sent to New York for nationwide distribution. Stories of an unusual nature were always forwarded. Within minutes, the story came back on the A wire, the main wire that major newspapers throughout the country used. Stories were then formatted in newspaper column width with justified margins on the teletypesetter wire, to which the smaller newspapers subscribed.

Later that day I talked with fire investigators to see if they had determined a cause of the fire. The investigator said the fire started in a couch that had a Naugahyde covering.

The first thing I did when I stepped into the house that afternoon was to check the couch in my living room. It had a Naugahyde covering, or at least that is what it said on that label you're not supposed to tear off. I didn't tear off the label, but I did cut a small piece from the back of the couch. I was curious as to whether it would really burn.

The next morning when we had a few minutes of free time, I took the piece of tan Naugahyde out of my shirt pocket. Ashtrays in the office at that time were usually full of ashes and cigarette butts. I had to clean the ashtray out and wash it before I could use it.

I tried to light the Naugahyde with a cigarette lighter, but it wouldn't catch.

"John! Be careful!" Sandi yelled from across the desk.

"This came from the back of my couch," I said. "It's Naugahyde, like what was on that couch in that girl's room at OSU."

I tried several times to light the Naugahyde without success.

"Maybe the fire didn't start in the couch," I said.

"You don't have all that stuffing that was behind it either," Sandi offered.

The Naugahyde didn't burn, and I never once thought about what would have happened had some of that clutter on the desks caught fire. We might have had our own disaster. Newspapers, copies of the day's stories, a used coffee cup that doubled as an ashtray, envelopes. How many days worth of paper? Beneath it all, an ashtray full of ashes and cigarette butts. People who had to work at that end of the desk just pushed things aside and typed.

The attempt to get Naugahyde to burn was a lesson in investigative reporting. I always liked to share ideas with my coworkers. I think it made them better workers and reporters. I really don't condone cutting up furniture, but it was an experiment.

Chapter 12

Sandi

Summer 1968
Working Nights

Three months after I started, I was moved to the night shift, working 3:00 p.m. to 11:00 p.m. on the broadcast desk. One of the jobs the broadcast people did on that shift was punch tape. Teletype operators, according to their contract, did not have to punch on TTY machines after 6:00 p.m. TTY machines were what fed the wire copy into broadcast stations. TTS was the machine that carried copy into newspapers, and it had justified margins to fit newspaper columns. Newspeople took over the job of punching tape from 6:00 p.m. to midnight. To help learn to punch tape, I had to learn to read it.

How am I ever going to learn to read tape? I was worried. To me it was a length of tape with holes in it. Dick O'Connell, one of the operators, made me a sample of five-level tape, where dots meant different letters. The ends of that pale yellow tape were fastened together to make a giant necklace that I wore as a cheat sheet until I learned my dot-based alphabet. It was like learning to read the Morse code. Each hole meant something. One hole could represent a letter, or a combination of holes could represent a letter. I still remember that all five holes were like an eraser. If you knew ahead of time you made a mistake while punching, you could go back and wipe it out with the key that made five holes and no keys on the teletype machine would strike paper.

My learning was broken down into three-month periods. I had the broadcast wire down pat in no time because that is where I came from. While working the broadcast shift, I watched and learned what was being done on the main desk. I was a little shaky when it came time to do it by myself.

Watching is one thing; doing it is another. If I made a mistake, I had a teletype operator to straighten me out. These men and a couple of women had been with UPI in the Columbus bureau for what seemed like forever. They knew a lot about writing news, only they didn't report; they typed—or rather, punched—our copy to send to the clients. They were vital to the operation in more ways than punching tape. These folks were walking encyclopedias, stylebooks, libraries, and morgues of archived stories, as well as friends and coworkers.

Some operators were nothing short of geniuses, especially at Christmastime. These were the people who created artwork with the teletype and transmitted it in the middle of the night. I marveled at the Christmas trees, parts of the nativity scene, an angel, or the Madonna. This artwork was generally vertical and always taped to the wall. One came out horizontal and was taped to the wall behind the A wire, the B wire, and the sports wire. That was Santa in his sleigh with his eight reindeer. What a work of art!

I had conquered the broadcast desk and was learning to run the main desk. Having only a few people on duty at any one time, we worked closely and grew together much as a family.

Those unusual hours had advantages and disadvantages. In the mornings I could drive to work with a minimum of traffic and usually be the first one in the parking lot. Not many people had to be at work at 6:00 a.m. If I had to be in at 3:00 p.m., traffic was light but I had difficulty finding a parking place. I would move my car close to the building at 6:00 p.m. when the parking lots emptied and the meters were free.

Having to be at work at 6:00 a.m. meant I had to get up around 4:00 a.m. I had to be in bed about the time everyone was getting started at evening activities. When I worked the second shift and got off at 11:00 p.m., everyone was in bed by the time I got home at around midnight. I wasn't ready to go to bed, so I stayed up and read. I found working these shifts was playing havoc with my social life. Joe and I began drifting apart.

I would have to make new friends. It was a little difficult, but I was determined to find a way.

One help was professional organizations. As a sophomore in college, I joined Theta Sigma Phi, which is a journalism honorary today known as Association of Women in Communications. I had been a member of Business and Professional Women and American Women in Radio and Television since shortly after I graduated from college. I could associate with other working women, both in my field and in other fields. That led me to new contacts that would prove helpful at work and create friendships away from the office that lasted for many years.

Chapter 13

John
June 1968
Jay Comes on Board

After we made it through a hectic week in May, I suddenly had an opening on my staff. Going through my file of applicants, I chose Jay Gibian, a general assignment reporter at the *Columbus Dispatch*, the city's afternoon newspaper. He, like Sandi, had some broadcast experience in his background.

Bringing on people from a radio station or a newspaper with a few years of experience proved valuable. They had been on the receiving end of the operations of a wire service and didn't require much training. I could let them work by themselves within days of their hiring.

They also brought with them a wealth of resources that they could tap when it came to covering a story. One thing Sandi had that Jay didn't was a knowledge of sports. But Jay was active with the police auxiliary in Columbus.

The day I announced Jay's hiring to the staff, Sandi popped in my office at the end of her shift.

"So, you're hiring Jay Gibian," she said, leaning against the doorjamb.

"You know him?" I asked.

"No, I don't know him, but I do know about him," she said.

"Oh?"

"Last fall when I was covering that missing girl in Delaware, the *Dispatch* assigned him to write a story one day," she related. "He and the police chief had an encounter on the phone and the chief hung up on him. Jay wrote a story about the chief hanging up. I don't know what the conversation was about, but apparently it wasn't going Jay's way."

"Let's hope he's calmed down by now," I said, tucking the information into the back of my mind.

When Jay started, he was assigned the day broadcast shift, and that pushed Sandi to nightside, where she adapted quickly to those operations as well as learning to operate the night news desk.

Chapter 14

Sandi
July 1968
Cleveland Riots

One quiet evening in late July, I was walking past the teletype machine where Cleveland and Cincinnati sent their stories to us. I heard the clacking and stopped to read what was coming.

"Jesus Christ," I yelled, drawing out the syllables. "Two Cleveland cops shot and killed. Did either of you hear bells?" I shouted to the two men working with me, Mason on the news desk and George Thomas, the teletype operator punching tape for the newspaper wire. They shook their heads.

I grabbed a copy of the story, ran around to the broadcast desk, and started to type a broadcast version. "Get Pittsburgh's attention and get some help on this one."

Mason called John before he called Pittsburgh. Columbus was a line bureau and had to rely on the division point—in our area it was Pittsburgh—to send the copy to New York. Pittsburgh was the regional hub and could send stories out of Ohio to New York for the national wire.

"I can't believe she sent that item down without bells," I said of the woman working in the Cleveland office. That was one of the few times I ever criticized a coworker.

Big stories were sent with a *bulletin* or *urgent* status and came with bells to get people's attention in newsrooms. Two police officers killed is a big story. This was also the start of a big story.

Within the hour, four black militants and three police officers were dead. These shootings touched off more violence, looting, an arson fire, and beatings that lasted for two days and nights.

Chapter 15

John
July 1968
Cleveland Riots

M ason called me to tell me two police officers had been shot and killed in the Glenville section of Cleveland.

One story of the start had it that black militant Ahmad Evans allegedly stole cars and parked them in Glenville, and then called police to tell them where the stolen cars were. When police arrived, Evans and his followers opened fire. Two police officers were killed in the opening barrage. Fires and looting followed. Within an hour, three police officers and four black activists were dead.

I knew this was more than the small Cleveland bureau could handle. I called on Dick Wheeler and Jay Gibian, who had asked to go, to augment our Cleveland coverage. I figured his experience with police and reporting would be beneficial.

Jay wanted to drive to where the shooting had occurred, but Dick didn't want to get shot at. Dick called me for advice. I told him to settle it and get the story. They went in. Shots were still being fired, and the two crept under the car for protection.

They had great quotes and information for the main story and sidebars that they phoned to me in Columbus. I cleaned up their copy and forwarded it to national via Pittsburgh.

Cleveland was just another city that experienced violence in a year that would go down in history as one of the most violent.

Less than a month later, violence came to Columbus, this time at the Ohio Penitentiary, where prisoners held in overcrowded cell blocks took nine guards hostage. The Ohio Highway Patrol and Ohio National Guard were summoned to assist Columbus police officers and prison guards in putting down the disturbance.

Here again I called upon the team of Wheeler and Gibian. I had a summer intern—Sue Reisinger—and I sent her down the second day of the riot, when it appeared law enforcement would make a dramatic move. She sat in an office in the Belmont Casket Company across the street holding a phone line open.

I heard her shout into the phone about the time I heard a blast—"They killed all the hostages!"

I couldn't confirm it from monitoring local radio stations and other reporters, and I didn't want to go with it without confirmation. Ted Virostko, who was now working next door for Scripps-Howard, could hear through a small square hole in the wall between our offices. He stuck his head through that small square and yelled, "John, the hostages are still alive." I'm glad I didn't run with that report without verification. I guess I could borrow a phrase from Sandi, who said it was easier to raise a death toll than play God and resurrect bodies.

The Highway Patrol and the National Guard had blasted a hole in the wall. Dick had run to Belmont Casket, where Sue was holding a telephone line open to the bureau, so he could report as things were happening. Jay, whom I sent over to do some color reporting for sidebars, hadn't wanted to leave a small building attached to the side of the prison but was persuaded to leave moments before the blast. The explosion's impact tossed around trophies that had been displayed from prisoner intramural competitions. Had Jay stayed, I'm sure he would have been injured.

The prison riot lasted two days—Wednesday and Thursday. Sandi was working a night broadcast shift, and I asked her to come in those two nights on her days off. She readily agreed. I didn't realize she had had tickets for a couple of theatrical presentations. She gave those away and came into work. The following week, she worked Sunday through Thursday. I didn't realize at the time how many consecutive days she worked until much later when she casually mentioned that once she had worked seventeen straight days and was really glad for a couple of days off.

Chapter 16

Sandi

Fall 1968

The Tigers Win!

I had been a Detroit Tigers fan since the spring of 1956. I was only twelve years old and had been allowed to stay home by myself one evening. I turned on my parents' radio and instead of getting music on WJR out of Detroit, I got a baseball game. Detroit beat Washington and I was hooked.

It wasn't long until I discovered I was beating a dead horse rooting for the Tigers, who were mired toward the bottom of the American League for many seasons. My love of sports, baseball, and the Tigers combined to lead me to want to become a baseball announcer. That's when my Dad told me if I wanted to become a baseball announcer, I had to learn journalism.

In 1967 the Tigers battled the Boston Red Sox down to the wire for the American League championship. In 1968, they picked up where they left off, winning the pennant on my birthday, with Columbus, Ohio, native Joe Sparma winning the game.

I was going to the World Series. Only I didn't understand the procedure to get tickets.

I had a weekend off, and the Tigers were playing the St. Louis Cardinals at home in games 4 and 5. I made my flight reservations, packed a change of clothes in an overnight bag that doubled as a purse, and set out for Detroit.

I had no tickets for the games and I didn't have lodging for Saturday night. But I did have a return flight. I bummed around the stadium and finally got my hands on standing-room-only tickets for both games. I could hardly see, but I could hear and what I was hearing wasn't the greatest. I found a room Saturday night at a fleabag hotel in downtown Detroit not far from Tiger Stadium.

Sunday's game was about as dreary as Saturday's. I flew back to Columbus dejected, and the Tigers went into St. Louis down three games to two.

Things began to look better in St. Louis. The Tigers tied the Series at three games each Tuesday and won it all Wednesday.

At least I could say I had been at a World Series game. Too bad the Tigers couldn't have won it when I was in the crowd.

Chapter 17

John
1969
New Year, New People

Celebrating the New Year—1969—meant some staff changes. Dick Lighter decided it was time to move on. That allowed me to name Dick Wheeler full-time in our Statehouse bureau. I hated to lose a solid desk person on the overnight or third shift.

For a replacement, I tapped into resources within the company. I learned that Lee Leonard in the Harrisburg, Pennsylvania, bureau was available. That was a legislative reporting job, and I could use him in Columbus. It wasn't long after Lee arrived that he took charge of our Statehouse bureau, with Wheeler being able to double in the office.

Betty Work was another versatile staffer, working both the night desk and overnight, often when regulars had nights off. She also doubled on rewrite. Betty was a young woman about Sandi's age, and Rick's girlfriend. Both Rick and Betty had gone to Ohio State's journalism school. Betty still resembled a lot of college students at this time—long straight hair halfway down her back and short skirts.

Once again I had a solid staff. I had a good crew. They knew what was needed and did it well. Sandi showed me she could handle all of the shifts and desks. She could write for newspapers as well as for broadcast, and she knew sports. She'd pick up the phone and do interviews between broadcast splits. It wasn't unusual for her to write for both print and broadcast and do a sports story all on the same shift. Since she was single and didn't have that big of a family—a mother and stepfather in Bucyrus and a brother in the navy—she was always willing to work holidays so her colleagues could enjoy the day with family. Those are reasons I scheduled her to work the third shift Friday, July 4, 1969.

It was part of a long weekend, and the Columbus people who were not working that weekend were out of state. Those who had to work were assigned twelve-hour shifts. Bad weather started coming in across Lake Erie about six o'clock, the start of Sandi's shift. This storm started in the Toledo area and worsened as it moved east. The storm whipped up tornadoes and heavy rain across northern Ohio, wiping out fireworks displays in many areas.

I had been in touch with Sandi early in the evening, not long after she started her shift. She said things were under control—nothing going on, a typical quiet holiday evening. She told me she was ahead of schedule for the work she had to get done for the rest of the night. I went to bed. I would relieve her at 6:00 a.m. A few hours later, she called to tell me the weather had worsened.

"Tornadoes hit in north central and northeast Ohio near Lake Erie," she said. "About 250 small boats were out on Lake Erie. Rhodes is going to fly over at daybreak."

"Who's in Cleveland?" I asked groggily.

"John Spetz. I told him to stay until all the boats were accounted for. He didn't particularly like it, but I said much needed to be done and I couldn't do it alone," she said.

"You handled that right," I told her.

I knew immediately Sandi needed help. Not much could be done in the middle of the night except preparations for what would take place at dawn. The National Guard had been summoned to help the stricken communities. The story was becoming too much for one person to handle, regardless of how competent that person was. I got dressed and went into the office as quickly as I could.

"You're going to have to fly with the governor," I told her when I arrived not long after her call. "You're the only person I have at this hour."

She sipped the coffee I brought her and made notes about the flooding, then wrote the morning's first broadcast split. Meanwhile, I called for a photographer and got Tom Wilcox from the *Columbus Citizen-Journal*. That was a Scripps-Howard newspaper, and E. W. Scripps and Roy Howard had founded United Press in 1907. We shared the photographers. He would fly with the governor, and we would use his photos.

Sandi and Tom left for the airport. The governor's entourage was flying from Don Scott, the airport operated by OSU.

I heard from Sandi when the group landed in Willoughby, a suburb east of Cleveland.

"The governor walked down a street in Cleveland," she said. "A tree had fallen on a convertible. He poked under the leaves and limbs of that car as if he were looking for a body."

She continued to tell me more of what had happened and what she had seen. "The floodwaters look like someone spilled coffee all over" was a description she used about an aerial view.

"Got to go," she said abruptly. "I'll call from the next stop. The governor bought everyone two cheeseburgers with the works. And we're getting ready to move on."

The next I heard from Sandi, she was in Port Clinton, close to Sandusky to the west. Again she started telling me what the governor had seen, what he had done, what he had told the people affected by the storms. At one point I heard her say thanks to someone. "That," she said, "was for the guy who handed me a bottle of pop. The governor plugged nickels in the pop cooler and bought everyone a drink. I needed that."

She returned to the office, wrote her story, pitched in to help Chris Graham on broadcast, and made a call to friends to see if she could spend the night in their spare room. She would be back the next morning for her regularly scheduled shift. She had already worked twenty-four hours and would put in another full day on Sunday.

Chapter 18

Sandi

Summer 1969
Life Continues Despite Disaster

I hadn't had fresh clothes since Friday afternoon, nearly fifty hours earlier. When I got home Sunday evening and slipped out of that skirt and blouse, I thought they would stand by themselves with all the sweat and dirt.

By Monday, everyone else was back on the job and taking over from the few of us who had worked so hard the past few days. I deserved my days off.

I returned to work a couple of days later, and it was as if nothing had happened. Floodwaters were receding, cleanup was going on, and work in a busy newsroom was getting back to normal. Flood stories had diminished to a few paragraphs in newspapers and toward the bottom of the broadcast reports. In all, forty-one people died, more than five hundred people were injured, more than ten thousand homes were damaged, and 104 small businesses were destroyed.

When big stories break, the usual work still has to be done in a newsroom. The rest of the world continues to go on as though nothing is happening elsewhere. While some people are concentrating on the breaking and continuing story, others have to do the daily tasks.

Whether it was street riots in Cleveland or floods and tornadoes in northeastern Ohio, we still received the regular morning phone calls from correspondents or stringers from around the state. We still had to provide news for the newspapers and radio and TV stations that didn't devote that much time and space to the major story. Mail came in every morning. Market reports came in every Monday through Friday. Weather forecasts needed to be transmitted to radio and TV stations four times a day. For instance, a radio station that focuses on agriculture wants its market reports on time to meet its schedule because such reports on that station are paid for by advertisers.

Even though I didn't get sent out on assignment much, I did many of the daily newsroom duties. I loved it. And I didn't envy those who went out. I knew what was expected and I did it, keeping my cool. My turn would come.

Chapter 19

John
July 1969
Mrs. Armstrong's Apple Dumplings

Despite the violence and bad weather in 1969, the big story at the end of the year was the United States putting a man on the moon.

This story had real meaning in Ohio because Neil Armstrong, the astronaut selected to be the first man on the lunar surface, was a native of Ohio, and his parents still lived in the little northwestern Ohio town of Wapakoneta.

We started making contact with the elder Armstrongs as soon as their son was chosen. I was serving as state editor at the time, and Carl Miller had come on board as bureau manager. We decided Carl would be the main person to be in Wapakoneta during launch time, and Sue Reisinger, back for her second summer as an intern, would go along for sidebars. Meanwhile, I moved over to run the daily operations on the main desk.

Carl and Sue called in daily stories on the family and town during the mission.

Just prior to launch day, I placed a call to the Armstrong household and talked with Neil's mother, Violet.

"What did you say to Neil in that last phone call?" I asked.

"I told him to hurry home and I'd make his favorite dessert," she told me.

"And what is that?" I asked.

"It's apple dumplings," she said.

"And how do you make them?" I queried.

She gave me her step-by-step directions of how she made apple dumplings. I was typing as fast as I could.

I wrote a little story, included her recipe, and sent it to New York, which immediately brought it back on the A wire.

A few days later, I found notes on the message wire or got a phone call from another bureau that this paper or that one used the apple dumplings story. It had play in many newspapers throughout the world.

I never got into the habit of saving copies of stories as some reporters did. I wrote so many bylined stories that had I saved them, I would have had a huge stack. I had decided this would be my last job, and I wouldn't need them for a portfolio.

Chapter 20

Sandi
Summer 1969
Columbus Riots

The third week in July 1969 was a busy one. *Apollo 11*, carrying Ohio-born astronaut Neil Armstrong to the moon, had blasted off July 20 from Cape Canaveral.

We were down two people with Carl Miller and Sue Reisinger in Wapakoneta. I was working night broadcast. Much to my surprise, I had come to enjoy the night shift. I didn't have to rely on an alarm clock.

The *Apollo 11* mission seemed like any other launch until the spacecraft began its lunar orbit.

I tuned one ear and one eye to the major space story, but the other ear and eye were on the local goings-on.

About a mile east of downtown is a strong African American community that had once been a thriving community. Businesses had flourished. Some homes had welcomed jazz musicians and dancing. The construction of Interstate 71 in the 1960s divided the community.

In this community, near Children's Hospital on the Near East side, a white man who owned a dry cleaning establishment allegedly shot and killed a black man. That was the spark that set off a couple of days of fire bombings, shootings, and looting. The Ohio National Guard was summoned to help the Columbus police.

John, thinking of Jay's strong reporting skills from his days at the local afternoon paper coupled with his affiliation with the police auxiliary, sent him out onto the streets to get information for stories.

When he came in that evening, he was pale, his skin almost as white as the police auxiliary cap he often wore. He was obviously shaken.

"I ducked behind a car when shooting began," he said. "Next thing I know a body rolls under the car."

He had witnessed the second shooting death in that area in as many days. I don't think he ever again asked to be sent out of the office on a story.

Chapter 21

Sandi
1969
Move to Columbus

I turned twenty-five late in 1968. It was a milestone year, and time to take stock of where I was. I'd been out of college a little more than three years and was in my third job. I'd worked at two small radio stations and now was handling news for a worldwide operating company. *Not bad*, I thought.

The year 1968 was filled with violence. I was glad to enter 1969. Maybe things would be better.

I was still living in Delaware, driving thirty miles a day to work. I was working nights and loving it, but it left me with few friends.

Early in 1969, UPI and the Wire Service Guild reached an agreement on a three-year contract. To me, it meant my annual pay would surpass $10,000. I was happy. I looked back to the days in my first full-time job in broadcasting, where I was making little more than a dollar an hour. In Delaware, my take-home pay had been $57.79 a week.

My bragging to my stepdad didn't seem to sit well. When I told him about the contract and what the pay meant to me, I still remember his response: "I've worked all my life and never made that kind of money." He was a foreman in a plant in central Ohio that made farm wagons.

Driving long distances, especially late at night, was beginning to get to me. I decided it was time to make the move to Columbus.

I had hesitated at first because I figured I was replacing someone who was going on active duty in the military and would be gone a year or so and then I'd be out of a job when he returned. That wasn't the case, but I also didn't know how long I'd be in this job.

Finances also concerned me. By late 1969, I had paid off the car I bought in January 1966. It was still in good condition. I could save money there.

I finally made the decision to move to Columbus. I searched for an inexpensive place to live, figuring I could make an initial move and worry about long-range living later.

I found a little apartment not far from some longtime family friends and settled in. I figured if I was close to someone I knew, I'd be safe and my mother and stepdad wouldn't have to worry about me.

Without checking where any of my UPI coworkers lived, I moved into Columbus. I didn't realize at the time that I had moved into John Kady's zip code.

Chapter 22

John
Winter 1969
Coal Mining in the Tri-State Area

I grew up in the northern panhandle of West Virginia in the heart of the coal mining district. Most of my friends and classmates were children of coal miners. An underground coal mine was across the road from my high school. The Hitchman Mine was next door to our baseball field, and so much coal dust settled on the field that we called it the Black Diamond.

Not far away was a store where the miners did their shopping. They could buy food and clothing using scrip that the mine paid them instead of dollars like Dad had when he'd get paid and cash his check. I didn't realize it then, but that store was a company store. I thought of it later when Tennessee Ernie Ford sang *Sixteen Tons*. The houses the miners lived in were company houses close to the Hitchman Mine, and the area was known as Hitchman's Row.

I didn't know until years later that the miners weren't treated well. What the miners received in scrip wasn't worth nearly as much as what they would have received had they been paid in real dollars. I'm glad my father was educated and had a good job and that he and Mom wanted all of us kids to do well.

The mines employed many people of different nationalities, and we had students of various ethnicities, much like the early twenty-first century in Columbus, with its large population of Somali, Latinos, and Hispanics and the international students who attend central Ohio colleges and universities. They brought their languages with them then, just as they do today. It seemed that English was a foreign language in my school.

I felt I knew the coal miners pretty well by the time I became a journalist. Life for them had improved quite a bit over the years, especially with the United Mine Workers (UMW) union that was formed in 1890 in Columbus, just a few blocks from the UPI offices.

John L. Lewis led the union for forty years, until his retirement in 1960. Two men served in that office after him, and the incumbent, Tony Boyle, was seeking reelection in 1969.

In the summer of 1969, Joseph "Jock" Yablonski announced his intention to run against Boyle. He believed corruption was prevalent within the union. Yablonski was recruited to run against Boyle by Miners for Democracy, led by John Guzek, which had pushed for opposition to the incumbent.

This faction of the UMW was headquartered in southeastern Ohio near the Ohio River in a town called Dilles Bottom. I always got a kick out of the top people in our Pittsburgh office saying, when we wrote stories from outlying areas, "Where does Kady come up with these datelines?"

Yablonski lost the election decisively in December.

Early in the new year, 1970, when Yablonski's son, Chip, hadn't heard from his family for a few days, he drove to their home in Clarksville, Pennsylvania. He found the bodies of his father, his mother, Margaret, and his sister, Charlotte. All had been shot.

The initial investigation revealed a car with Ohio license plates had been seen in the area the apparent day of the shootings, New Year's Eve 1969. The investigation led to several arrests a few weeks later.

This was destined to be a story we would write for a long time to come.

Chapter 23

Sandi

Early 1970
Yablonski Arrests

When I worked the night desk, I'd take a lunch break at six in the evening. This had long been my routine. Mason Blosser, who worked the night desk when I started working nights, would take his lunch hour—or was it dinner hour?—at that time. Quite often, I went to Paoletti's, an Italian restaurant around the corner across from the Statehouse. Sports reporters from the *Columbus Citizen-Journal*, the morning newspaper, took their lunch break at the same time, and I would join them at their table.

That's what happened the night of January 22, 1970. When I returned, Chris Graham on broadcast took his break, also going to Paoletti's. George Thomas, like most of our teletype operators, carried a lunch and ate when their work slowed. That night George caught a story coming out of Pittsburgh and called my attention to it.

"Oh my God! They arrested someone for the Yablonski killings," I said. Only George heard me. Chris was at lunch.

The FBI in Cleveland had arrested Paul Gilly, Aubran "Buddy" Martin, and Claude Vealey in the deaths of Joseph Yablonski and his wife and daughter on New Year's Eve. It hadn't taken long to identify the suspects. After all, they tossed beer cans out of their car while still on the Yablonski property. Those cans were covered with fingerprints!

George had picked the story off the western Pennsylvania/West Virginia newspaper wire and put it on the Ohio newspaper wire. I think it was the first time I saw him leave his area and venture to the other side of the room. He made sure the story was moving on the Metro wire that Cleveland and Cincinnati read. That was a help. I was getting the story on the broadcast wire. I also had to make sure photos were running. It seemed as if I was going in all directions at once.

This was a big story, and here I was handling it alone. It was around seven thirty and a big hour for stories, a good time to get a breaking story out for newspapers to get a good position on the front page and a good time for a story on the broadcast wire so television stations could plan for strong coverage at the 11:00 p.m. newscasts.

By the time Chris returned from lunch at eight, I had the phone at the photographer's desk at one ear talking with the FBI in Cleveland, and the phone at the sports desk at the other ear, talking with the Cleveland bureau. I was blocking Chris from going to the coatrack to hang up his jacket. I raised my right leg and used it to point to the A wire. He looked at the A wire and mouthed "broadcast," and I nodded. He put his hands on my shoulders, planted a kiss on my forehead, said "good work," and headed to his desk. First time I had that kind of thank-you for a job well done. At least he had some fresh copy to work with for the rest of the night.

With three bureaus working the story, we had much to do. Who were these people? What was their connection to the UMW? Where were they being held? What was in store for them? Who's writing what story? We worked as much as we could that night, and the folks the next day took over.

It wasn't long before Paul Gilly's wife, Annette, her father, Silous Huddleston of Tennessee, and another man, William Prater, were arrested. Prater and Albert Pass, who was also arrested a short time later, were officials of UMW District 21 in Kentucky.

By this time I knew we would be writing a Yablonski story forever. The suspects were all convicted by 1972 and sentenced to prison.

A federal investigation was launched on the basis of Yablonski's allegations of Tony Boyle's mishandling of union funds. During the trials and the investigation, it was determined that Boyle had embezzled and misused union funds, including to pay for the killings as well as for a reward to find the killers. Boyle was convicted of embezzling union funds to make illegal campaign contributions, and also murder. He was sentenced to prison where he died.

The union had fought for job health and safety for the miners and scored several victories. But in the early 1970s, the newly formed Environmental Protection Agency worked toward passage of clean air and clean water acts. Those laws sent companies in search of fuels alternative to coal. They also led to a loss of jobs in the mining industry. In later years, the UMW was recruiting members from other businesses.

Chapter 24

Sandi

Spring 1970
The Turbulent Sixties Come to an End

B y the spring of 1970, I had been at UPI for two years, longer than I thought I would be. When I was offered the job, I was under the impression that I would be replacing Rick Van Sant, who was waiting to be notified of his active duty status. When I started, I replaced Gloria Campisi, who transferred to the Philadelphia bureau. Three other vacancies opened before Rick received his notice in 1969. I had mastered all three shifts, as well as broadcast desk, the news desk, and rewrite. I wasn't that proficient at filing the newspaper wire on dayside, the task of the state editor. Maybe that was because I hadn't worked in a newspaper office and hadn't worked that particular desk more than once a month or so. I still loved coming to work every day.

I was assigned to work three months on the third-shift or overnight desk. Generally UPI worked an employee for three months on a particular desk, and then moved him or her to another desk or another shift. That way the person could learn all operations. I didn't mind working the different shifts. In fact, I liked the second shift. I didn't have to rely on an alarm clock and I could stay up as late as I wanted, but it did cut into my social life. One thing I didn't like about working third shift was the lack of things to do at seven o'clock in the morning. If

I needed groceries, I couldn't go to the store because it didn't open until nine or ten o'clock. Stores were not open around the clock yet. I hated going to bed at that hour. I guess I could read over breakfast. But what was breakfast? After working all night, do you eat a donut and drink a cup of coffee, or do you fix a traditional dinner? Broiling a hamburger or making macaroni and cheese at eight in the morning didn't seem right.

So much was going on that spring that left me on such a natural high at seven in the morning that it was difficult to wind down and go to sleep. A person working a regular shift doesn't go to bed when he or she gets home. It seems our bodies are programmed for sleep when it gets dark. I didn't start getting tired until the stores opened. It was hard to sleep during the day with sunlight coming through the windows, even though the blinds and curtains or drapes were pulled.

One of the big stories that spring was the height of student unrest on college campuses. The Vietnam War was unpopular, and young people were protesting the American involvement that had gone on longer than either the Civil War or World War II.

As temperatures climbed, so did the number of student demonstrations. It wasn't long until the Ohio National Guard was summoned to quiet the demonstrators. The call from the adjutant general's office would come about three o'clock in the morning, just about when I had time for a break.

The calls came so frequently that the caller from the adjutant general's office knew me pretty well.

"Sandi, we're calling out the Guard again," he would say.

I would get the information about what units and from what cities, and about where they were to go and what they would be doing, write the bulletins, and call Carl Miller, then our bureau manager. He would come in as soon as he could to provide an extra hand, as well as get a head start on the dayside work.

That spring the National Guard was called out not only for student unrest on campuses, but also to help provide safe traveling for steel haulers. The steel haulers, who had broken away from the Teamsters Union, were trying to get a contract with Republic Steel to replace the striking Teamsters. The dissidents formed the Fraternal Association of Steel Haulers (FASH), and this resulted in clashes on the Ohio Turnpike, especially at Exit 5 near Republic Steel. Shots were fired at some truckers.

The National Guard was called out eight times in the three months I worked the overnight. It was so frequent that the eighth time I had to call Carl in the middle of the night, he answered the phone with, "Okay, Sandi, where did you put the National Guard this time?"

That eighth time came in late April, when the Guard was called out because of student unrest at Kent State University, my alma mater. It was also at the end of my three-month stint on that desk. I don't think the National Guard had ever been called out so frequently before. I know it wasn't my fault.

I was so happy to get off work that Friday morning. I was exhausted but excited about having a four-day weekend. Four whole days off! I was going to Cincinnati. It was one of the last times the Cincinnati Reds would be playing in Crosley Field, and I had never been to a Reds game. The Reds and Pittsburgh Pirates were playing a four-game series, with a doubleheader on Sunday. I was planning to return home Monday, May 4, and would be back to work Tuesday, an election day. The big race was Governor James A. Rhodes seeking the Republican nomination for the US Senate.

I kept up with the events of the weekend at Kent State. Student protestors had burned a ROTC building. I didn't like the idea of students rioting and burning buildings. The white-frame building had been erected during World War II. Four such buildings were being used when I started classes there in January 1962. At that time I understood those wooden buildings used for classrooms were temporary. Three were barracks-style buildings of two to three floors. The fourth served as headquarters for the ROTC. *If they were temporary buildings in the early 1940s, then why were they still standing some twenty years later?* I wondered. My first class winter quarter was an 8:00 a.m. Latin class in one of those buildings. They were cold in winter and hot with no air-conditioning in the spring. I thought it a blessing that building was destroyed. Secretly, I would have liked to have seen the others go, but I didn't advocate it. They could have been torn down rather than burned.

Sightseeing, ball games, meals with friends—it was a wonderful spring weekend in Cincinnati, a city I hadn't visited since my early college days.

Monday morning I stopped at the UPI office in Cincinnati. It was a hole-in-the-wall office, not much bigger than the little walk-in newsroom I had at WDLR radio. I've seen walk-in closets bigger than those rooms. Standing there talking to Terry Flynn, the bureau manager, I heard many bells from the teletype. Terry and I turned around, and I stared at the machine typing one letter after another. Four dead at Kent State.

I took off my glasses to wipe away a tear. How could this happen at my alma mater, a campus that held a sacred spot in my heart and mind?

Kent State was my school. It was the one I chose by myself when I was in high school. It was where I earned my education, learned so much about journalism, newspapers, and broadcasting, and where I was making small donations annually to the School of Journalism, the athletic department, and the alumni association.

"I have to get back to Columbus," I said, shaking Terry's hand. "They're going to need extra help."

In my little more than two years at UPI, I knew how much work would go into this story. I started to put my glasses back on as I walked toward the door, only to see the right earpiece fall off.

"Fine time for this to happen," I said as I made my way to the parking lot and my car. I kept my glasses on the best I could as I drove the hundred miles up Interstate 71 to Columbus.

"I need an eye examination anyway. I'll call tomorrow to schedule one."

Chapter 25

John
May 1970
More than Kent State

Governor James A. Rhodes had approved of the National Guard being sent to Kent State to put down the rioting and restore calm. I don't think he anticipated the results. I don't think anyone did.

The Guard, many not much older than the young people protesting the war a half a world away, opened fire.

And that action may have carried over to the ballot box the next day.

The shootings occurred on a Monday, the day before a primary election. Rhodes was in his last year of his second term and seeking the Republican nomination for the US Senate. He lost his bid for nomination, and the Republicans lost the seat in November.

The Kent State story shared top spot in news stories with the election. The election story died out a couple of days later, but the Kent State story continued.

It was one that would be written for a long time. Everyone who worked the main desk had to write a fresh story by seeking out new information. I was surprised one of those early days by Sandi's concerns.

"Are you going to trust me writing this story?" she asked. "You know how I feel about Kent State."

I knew all about her connections to Kent State, her loyalty to the school where she earned her education. She was always promoting Kent State and its good journalism school, one of the more well-respected schools in the state, perhaps even in the nation.

"You write the game stories on football and basketball with no problem," I told her. "You can do this just as well."

"Yeah, I can do the football and basketball stories all right," she quipped. "They don't win."

I was fortunate to have found and hired her. She could write almost anything I asked her to write. It's not often I could get a woman who could write sports, and that is one reason I could work her at nights and weekends.

On football Saturdays she would wear a blue pleated skirt, white shirt, and gold sweater she said she had knitted. She said it was her first project, and she did it as a sophomore in college. She looked like a cheerleader. We used to tease her about the colors. She maintained it was "my not Michigan outfit."

"Michigan colors are maize and blue," she said. "These are blue and gold."

I always got a laugh out of her descriptions.

"You can do it," I told her as she settled down to work the desk that day.

Sandi's versatility prompted me to talk to Carl about the possibility of giving her some special assignments.

"I'd like to see you do some feature stories," Carl said to her. "Let me see five and we'll decide about the regularity of such an assignment."

Five stories is generally what an editor will ask for when a person suggests writing a column or freelancing features at a magazine. His request wasn't out of the ordinary.

For her first story, she called the Marathon Oil Company in Findlay and talked with a woman she had heard not long before present a program to women on how to learn parts of cars and what role they have. Her lead explained the job of the manifold as a heater. She wrote something like, "If you're going on a long trip, wrap a pot roast in aluminum foil, tie it to the manifold, and the meat will be done when you reach your destination."

The story was well written, and I offered it to the national features desk in New York. Marathon Oil had a clip service and sent her copies of where the story appeared. The clip file was an inch or so thick!

Around the holidays she came through again with a story of how to care for poinsettias to keep them growing throughout the year so they would bloom again the following year. She interviewed someone with a Hispanic-sounding name who had come from South America. Again I offered the story to New York, and this time, she received clips from South America.

Although Dick Lightner was no longer working for UPI, I often thanked him for suggesting I offer her a job.

Chapter 26

John
Spring 1970
Dr. Sam

Right in the midst of the Yablonski murder investigation, steel haulers' protests, and campus unrest came yet another major story: the death of Dr. Sam Sheppard.

The one-time osteopath from the Cleveland suburb of Bay Village had been in the headlines quite a bit since his pregnant wife, Marilyn, was killed July 4, 1954.

He had been arrested, charged with murder, tried, convicted, and sentenced to the Ohio Penitentiary. Ten years later, his conviction was overturned, and he was acquitted in a second trial. Dr. Sam married German immigrant Arianne Tebbejohanns a few days after he was released from prison, but the marriage lasted only three years. He tried to get back into medicine, but a couple of malpractice suits cut short his medical career.

With a friend, he then turned to tag-team wrestling and even married his friend's daughter.

Then came April 6, 1970.

Ed DiPietro, UPI state editor, took a phone call that morning. It was the wife of Dr. Sam's wrestling partner, George Strickland. Dr. Sam had died.

Why she called UPI before calling police is something that remained a mystery, but I guess it pays to have connections or good sources.

After confirming the death, I could write the story from my head or my heart. UPI had followed the Sheppard case since 1954, and I read the files and helped write and edit the stories after the second trial.

The big question now was, *how did he die?*

I was working the news desk at the time. I called the county coroner's office and spoke politely with the secretary. She was quite rattled, knowing the office had such a newsworthy body. Maybe she wasn't used to fielding so many calls from the media. I asked her if she or her boss, Dr. Robert Evans, would call me when the autopsy report was ready.

One morning not long afterward I got a call from Dr. Evans, giving me the results of the autopsy. Just six months before his death, Sheppard, by now an alcoholic, had married Strickland's daughter Colleen. He was drinking heavily, as much as two fifths a day. Death was attributed to liver failure, according to the coroner.

At the time Dr. Evans called me that morning, several representatives of the media were sitting in the waiting room of his office.

I wrote the bulletin and followed it with an urgent story, what is known in the news business as a *1st lead writethru*, which is standard for a breaking story. Get the main points out quickly and follow with a rewritten story, pulling in as much as possible for newspapers on that cycle. And then a fresh story with new information follows for the next cycle. In this case, we got the story out for the PM papers and had a longer story for the morning papers. Much of that was used again for papers that published the next afternoon.

About an hour after I had spoken with Dr. Evans and our story was on the wire, I took a call from Jim Gravelle, news director at WCOL radio down the street, telling me he had a big story.

I asked him what it was and he started to tell me about the coroner's report on Dr. Sam.

"We had that an hour ago," I said.

"How'd you do that?" he asked.

"It's magic," I quipped.

It's not magic, really—just good manners.

Chapter 27

Sandi

Summer 1971
My Move to Lincoln Village

After living in the small apartment building in Columbus for little more than a year, I decided to move to a better location. I didn't like the way my neighborhood was going.

The neighbors weren't really the type I wanted to associate with, but that's what happens when rent is $100 or so a month. I was much better off than people who were moving in, and I didn't want to be associated with them.

I also wasn't sure about the management of the complex. Those in the office didn't seem too friendly when I dropped off my check each month. I wanted out.

I started looking for a new place to live. Not far away were a couple of apartment buildings surrounded by townhouses. In the middle were a swimming pool and a basketball court. This area was behind a strip shopping center with a library and a grocery store, two businesses I could hardly live without.

The day I moved in, I thought I heard someone call my name. I looked around but didn't see anyone. Sandi is a common name anyway.

Chapter 28

John

Summer 1971
Sandi Is My Neighbor

Joyce, the girls, and I were living in a townhouse on Tarryton Court East in Lincoln Village North in the late sixties and early seventies. I was coming out of the house late one afternoon to go shopping and saw Sandi—or at least I thought it was her—coming out of an apartment building about a football field's length west. From across the parking lot, I waved and shouted at her.

With our days off scheduled the way they were, I didn't see her again until midafternoon Thursday. She arrived early for her night broadcast shift, and I asked her, "Are you living in those apartments?"

"Yeah, I moved in during the weekend," she said. "Do you live there?"

Our townhouse was on the east side of the complex.

"You mean I can stick my head out of my window and watch your girls on the playground?"

"Did you know that Ruth and Bob live a couple of streets down the way?" I asked her.

"What is this?" she asked. "A UPI party on the west side?"

Ruth Bynum was a teletype operator whose two daughters were about the age of Jennifer and Gretchen. She was divorced and raising

96

her two girls. Bob Grimm had been the UPI sportswriter for Ohio for twenty years, retiring at the end of 1968 and going to work at the Ohio Education Association. They both lived on the same street, less than a mile away from Sandi and me.

In the summer, Joyce was a lifeguard at the pool, and Jennifer and Gretchen played on the basketball court.

I had to bum a ride with someone or take a cab to work because I didn't have a driver's license. Thank goodness a couple of coworkers—Ruth and Sandi—lived close by and worked about the same shift I did. I could go in with either one of them and pay the parking fee in the garage under the Statehouse.

I'd had a driver's license when I arrived in Columbus in January 1967. About six months later, a police officer stopped me on West Broad Street on my way home from work. He said I had run a red light. West Broad Street is US Route 40, the original National Road, a major east-west artery through the city. The officer asked for my license, the car registration, and my proof of insurance. I had all that, only my license was from Kentucky and I had been in Ohio long enough for it to be renewed from Ohio. I had to go to court.

I hired an attorney, Joe Hahn, but when the judge found out I worked for UPI, he began lecturing me about newspaper editorials about judges being soft on crime. I tried to explain that I didn't write the editorials, that UPI didn't provide the editorials, that they were written by the individual newspapers. That's when my attorney asked for a recess, during which he told me to keep my mouth shut and not argue with the judge.

I lost my case. I didn't have a valid driver's license and was fined $50. I had to start all over, taking a driver's test. I flunked it. Joyce's driver's license was also from Kentucky and it was expired. She too flunked her test.

So our Oldsmobile 98 sat out in front of our townhouse for about a year until we sold it.

I didn't get my driver's license again until 1974.

One morning when Sandi drove across the parking lot to pick me up, I opened the door of her blue Buick and was about to plop down on the front seat when she yelled, "Hold it." She reached over and grabbed her white Tupperware container.

"Here, hold this," she said, handing the container to me as I carefully sat down.

"What is this?"

"I made a strawberry pie last night," she said. "We'll have it with coffee when we get to work."

Sandi and I often rode to work together. It would be about daybreak when we were climbing the steps to Broad and High streets, the heart of downtown Columbus. The stairwells usually reeked with the strong putrid smell of urine.

"Oh my God, John," she gasped one morning and grabbed my elbow.

"What's up, babe?"

"I almost stepped on a sleeping wino." She let out a loud breath and continued up the steps.

Homeless men sleeping in the stairwells were just part of the scenery the first block of downtown. A concrete wall ran along the Broad Street side of the Statehouse lawn and provided a leaning post for scantily clad women, who tried to entice the many male passersby, even in the morning rush hour.

Street people could be found across the street in front of the office buildings and Jack and Benny's restaurant, which was open around the clock.

By the time the working crowd began swarming into downtown, the street people had started gathering. The Rev. Paul Shaver was a mainstay near the door of the building housing the UPI offices. He waved his well-worn black-cover Bible above his head, warning people they would go to eternal damnation if they didn't repent.

And who could forget Pinky? He was a skinny little fellow who always dressed in a pastel pink leisure suit. I often encountered him on the northeast corner of Broad and High in front of the old Roys Jewelers store. He would wave and say hi to all who passed by.

It was not unusual to stumble over the legs of an itinerant musician, who'd sit on the sidewalk playing a guitar and hoping people would drop a few coins into a hat or his guitar box.

As we were accustomed to these diversions, we knew they wouldn't harm anyone, but to be on the safe side in the afternoons, we always walked as close to the curb as possible to the office building less than a block away.

Having Sunday and Monday off meant I had to work Saturday. It was a quiet time and I could always get my paperwork done. I made out the schedules for the news side and conferred with the chief teletype operator about who would be working the Saturday shift. Saturdays are a different type of day. When much of the news is generated by people working in an office, things almost come to a halt when those offices are closed.

Most restaurants were open Monday through Friday, doing business for those who worked downtown on weekdays. The major department store, Lazarus, maintained a couple of restaurants. Down the street was Jack and Benny's, the long-standing short-order restaurant with big cheeseburgers and meringue-topped pies. A couple of blocks the other way was the first Wendy's restaurant. A few blocks away was a White Castle, another twenty-four-hour fast-food restaurant, home of the little square burger smothered in onions that was known as the slider.

That didn't leave many options for lunch on the weekends. Often during the week, we'd bring in the previous night's leftovers for lunch. Or should I say breakfast? Our early-morning stringer callers knew us pretty well. When I worked with Sandi, I could hear her tell those callers about the food. "I'm working my way through shrimp Creole," or "John brought in stuffed zucchini."

With a reduced workload on Saturday, we didn't have as many people working as we did during the week. I checked with the teletype operators on their schedule, and it seemed we had a different group every Saturday. So we'd bring in food.

Our kitchen supplies were meager. I could warm up the previous night's leftovers in the toaster oven. Ron Hill, one of the operators, concocted a way to make coffee. He turned a drab army-green cylindrical metal trash can upside down. On top of that was a one-burner hot plate that alternated ceramic and wire coils that glowed orange when the fabric-covered cord was plugged in. He found a lumber-camp type of pot to brew the coffee. It was often so strong it could have peeled the paint off the walls.

That was the same setup where another operator, Phil Argento, heated his spaghetti sauce. I didn't ask for the recipe, but I always wondered if it had a secret ingredient. He brought in fresh Parmesan cheese and grated it over everyone's servings.

Everyone had a good time participating in our Saturday feasts except Jay. He didn't like the idea of people eating at the work site. He would work straight through without taking a break for lunch and leave an hour early.

One day I brought the night before's leftover fried chicken for my lunch. When I finished work for the day, I dropped the bones into the typewriter so that when Jay took over the night desk and started typing, the chicken bones would go flying. He let me know later that night he didn't appreciate what I did.

We always had food in the office. Many of us would bring our lunch. One time when Rhodes was governor, I brought in a jar of limburger and a bunch of green onions. I was snacking away when Jim Duerk, the governor's press secretary, walked in with a news release.

"I see it but I don't believe it," he said as he turned to walk out. His boss always had food too, but more normal, I would say: a pot of vegetable soup, tomato juice, popcorn.

I always liked it when Sandi worked Saturdays. I knew she would bring in Swedish meatballs. On the way to work those mornings, I would hold her electric skillet with the meatballs. I could smell them even though they still had to be cooked. All other ingredients for the day's lunch were in a shopping bag. We had a dorm-sized refrigerator to hold the food until we started cooking about ten thirty in the morning, and her electric skillet just fit in there.

The first time she brought them, she didn't have any to take home for leftovers.

"Is this a family recipe?" was one comment.

"No," she said. "Last Christmas my brother in the navy was unable to get home for the holidays. I had invited Mom and my stepdad to dinner. I had this strange hankering for Swedish meatballs. I didn't even know what they were. The *Dispatch* food section just before Christmas carried a recipe for Swedish meatballs, so I tried it."

A couple of times when she worked, she provided a special dessert. One of her specialties was apple cream pie.

Sandi only worked dayside in spring and summer because she had become proficient at compiling football and basketball scores on Friday nights and anchored the Saturday afternoon football and basketball coverage in the office.

On Christmas Eve 1970, I allowed those who worked to bring in something to drink as long as they didn't abuse that privilege and did their work. The crew who worked New Year's Eve was a different group and I allowed them the same privilege.

Chapter 29

Sandi

Winter 1971

John Overdrinks

That decision probably was the worst one John ever made.

Chris Graham, who was working night broadcast, grabbed me by the shoulders the minute I stepped into the office to work the night desk beginning at 4:00 p.m.

"Don't go down to the ladies' room," he said. I looked at him quizzically. "John's down there."

"Why?" I asked.

"He finished off somebody's bottle of blackberry wine from this morning and we had to rescue him from the top floor of the building."

The ladies' room on the lower level was the only place that had a couch. A key to the room was in a drawer in the desk used by the broadcast staffer. John was down there sleeping it off.

I didn't think much more about it and went about my work. About an hour or so into my shift Joyce called, wanting to know where John was.

I stammered through some kind of lame excuse that John had met up with someone he hadn't seen for a while and the two of them were gone by the time I arrived and that the others on nightside didn't know where they went. I could tell she wasn't happy and that she probably didn't believe me. Somehow I had the feeling this wasn't the first time John was having trouble holding his liquor.

Chapter 30

John

Early 1971

Rhodes's Announcement

Competition is good. It keeps one on his or her toes. I found it also helps to know who is walking in to deliver a news release.

Jim Rhodes had served as governor from 1963 through 1970, two four-year terms.

Throughout most of Ohio history, the governor could serve an unlimited number of two-year terms. Around the middle of the twentieth century, the Ohio Constitution was changed to allow four-year terms and only two terms. In essence, he was term-limited.

Rhodes, who grew up in a poor area of southern Ohio, moved to Columbus and served in city and state offices before seeking higher office. Elected governor in 1962, he enjoyed being in office and he wanted to serve longer but was prohibited. The only way he could run again was to challenge the Constitution, and I was waiting for that.

I knew Fred Rice, director of the Bureau of Motor Vehicles, often helped deliver news releases from Rhodes, who, after his two terms as governor, opened a development office in a nearby building. One morning around eight o'clock, Rice popped into the office and dropped an envelope on the desk where I was sorting mail to see what had to be written.

Anxiously awaiting the announcement, I asked him, "Is this the big one?"

He didn't say anything, but he smiled, turned around, and walked out.

I opened the envelope, and yes, it was the big one I had been waiting for. Rhodes was seeking a court opinion on whether he could serve as governor again.

I put a "book" in the typewriter—a sheaf of four pages of paper with carbon between them. One copy went to the newspaper desk, one to the main desk, one to broadcast, and one to our neighbors at Scripps-Howard. I typed a one-paragraph *bulletin*, followed that with a couple of paragraphs as an *urgent*, and had the teletype operators send it out. Jay was working broadcast that day, and he was writing broadcast stories on the announcement at the same time.

I then reached into the bottom drawer, where I kept a stack of obituaries, and pulled out one for Rhodes. I crossed out a couple of paragraphs, wrote a transition paragraph, and sent the rest of the obit to the operators. This was midmorning, and we still had plenty of time to get the story to the afternoon newspapers. We had scrambled.

To me it was just another day on the job.

All that changed a couple of days later when the *Dayton Daily News* called and asked me what happened that morning. The newspaper was doing a story on how the wire services handled the big announcement.

The *Dayton Daily News* was a two-service paper at that time, receiving both UPI and AP stories. Its competition was the *Dayton Journal Herald*, which was a UPI-only paper. The *Dayton Daily News* received the UPI story of Rhodes's request for a court ruling but didn't see a story from the AP until the start of the next cycle, the one for newspapers that publish morning editions. "What happened?" was the paper's big question.

What happened that morning was that when Fred handed me the envelope, I opened it immediately, read the release, and wrote the story. Maybe what happened at the AP office around the corner was that when the desk person was handed the envelope containing the release, he put it at the bottom of the pile of mail and opened it when he got down to it.

By that time, it was too late for the afternoon papers, and the AP didn't realize that the UPI story had been on the wire for a long time. Those afternoon papers who were AP members got the story a day later. Most papers at that time were still afternoon editions and were put together in the morning and on the streets by midafternoon.

Within a week State Editor Ed DiPietro and Regional Executive Ron Wills—actually a salesperson—created a flyer that they sent to all newspapers and radio and TV stations in Ohio touting the quick work of John Kady and the UPI crew in getting this announcement out to our clients long before AP had it.

He won the challenge, with the Supreme Court saying he could seek the governorship again. He won in 1974 and ran again—and won—in 1978. In all, he served sixteen years, the longest serving governor in Ohio. He served four terms; Frank Lausche had served five terms, but he had two-year terms.

Most people remember Rhodes and his downfall by the Kent State shootings, but Rhodes said his biggest achievement was bringing Honda to Ohio to make cars.

Chapter 31

Sandi
May 1972
Election of 1972

Reporters need to develop good, trustworthy sources. I learned that early. When I was an area correspondent in junior high and high school, I knew the leaders of different groups, their phone numbers, and where they lived. They also knew my phone number and where I lived.

At college, newsmakers quickly found the student newspaper offices and stopped in frequently. We always kept a phone directory.

Reporters spend much of their time inside, writing stories newscasters read on the air or stories the readers see in the newspapers. Reporters don't know everything that is happening outside their buildings and rely on those sources.

Similarly, at a wire service, we reporters needed to cultivate a crop of sources throughout the state. This is where reporters at our client points—both print and broadcast—came to the rescue. We had some who would call every morning to let us know what was going on in their area. And when something major was breaking, they'd call us to tip us off. They were our stringers and got paid for their calls, but not enough to go into a higher tax bracket; it was more like extra spending money.

I was working day broadcast for Ohio's primary election day. It seemed like a normal start to any day. I handled the usual early morning calls; not much going on. About an hour into our shift, all that changed.

Voting machines in Cleveland didn't function properly, despite having passed a preelection test. This election was a big one. President Richard Nixon was considered a shoo-in for nomination for reelection on the Republican ticket. Names like George McGovern and Hubert Humphrey topped the Democratic list, with several minor candidates on Ohio's bedsheet ballot.

Within a short time of the malfunction being discovered, the primary election in Cuyahoga County, the state's most populous county, was called off. Residents were scheduled to vote the following Tuesday.

About the same time as we were dealing with that story, I took a call from Bill Clark, the news director from WKBN in Youngstown.

"Sandi," he began, "I took a call from an FBI special agent who said J. Edgar Hoover died during the night."

I stretched the phone cord as far as I could to read the latest on the broadcast wire. The death of the longtime director of the FBI would be the top story. It wasn't there.

"I went with it," Bill was saying. "But I haven't seen anything on the wire. What do you know?"

"Hang in there, Bill," I told him. "I'm on it."

I inserted a piece of copy paper into my typewriter and wrote out a message for Washington. I yelled for an operator. The operator on duty for the wire where we sent messages to Pittsburgh to relay to other bureaus punched it in and ran bells with it.

We waited. The longer we waited, the more anxious we got. About an hour later, the story came back, and I immediately called Bill Clark back and pointed out the story.

"Thank you, Sandi," he said. "I'm relieved. I was really sweating it for a while."

So were we.

Chapter 32

John
Spring 1972
Weather

O hio's weather is too hot, too cold, too windy, too rainy, too snowy, too something or other, but it makes for good stories.

Curt Taylor, one of our longtime teletype operators, always told us if we wrote about the weather, people's pocketbooks, or politics, newspapers would use the story.

In springtime, we were accustomed to fluctuating temperatures. It would be warm one day, cold the next, or vice versa. Early in my tenure, we were in a cold spell after some warm weather. I wanted to know how it affected the crops because agriculture was Ohio's top industry. At this time of the year, trees and plants were coming into bud.

As soon I arrived at the office, I placed a call to Bill Swank, vice president of the Ohio Farm Bureau Federation. I would often call him shortly after six in the morning.

"Is this too early to call you, Mr. Swank?" I asked politely on one of my first calls to him.

"No, John," he said. "I'm on my second cup of coffee."

I made many calls to Bill over the years. He always had good information, with lots of color. He kept in constant touch with the county extension agents and would give us thorough reports or leads and phone numbers to get in touch with people who would make good interviews for our stories. Jim Dible, editor of the *Tiffin Advertiser-Tribune* in northwest Ohio, always told me talking with Bill Swank was like talking to God.

After the snow melted and spring rains fell, rivers would run high. Many times I heard, "If you spit in the Scioto River at LaRue in Marion County, the river floods below Chillicothe." The Maumee, Grand, and Sandusky rivers flowed into Lake Erie, while the Scioto, Muskingum, Hocking, and Miami flowed south into the Ohio River.

Often high water from the Ohio rivers met high water rushing down from rivers in neighboring Pennsylvania to create flooding conditions along the Ohio River from the junction of Ohio, West Virginia, and Pennsylvania to where the Ohio flowed into the Mississippi at Cairo, Illinois.

In 1972, Hurricane Agnes roared through the upper mid-Atlantic states, pounding much of Pennsylvania with high winds and heavy rains. Rivers that flowed to the Ohio River were swollen and prompted evacuations. Our Pittsburgh office called me at home Saturday evening and said they needed a flood story out of Ohio the next day. Sandi was scheduled to work that Sunday morning, so I called and asked if I could hitch a ride with her. Normally she would be working by herself.

Just before she walked out of her apartment, she picked up what remained of a daffodil angel food cake she had made for a weekend potluck with friends. She handed the container to me as I got into her car.

"We'll have cake this morning," she said.

As Sandi concentrated on normal Sunday work of checking out-of-town newspapers, I set about working the phones for a flood story. One of my first calls was to Ruth Westlake, the managing editor of the *Martins Ferry Times Leader*. I could always count on her for a good story when water was high.

"Oh, you know, John, it's business as usual," she started out. "When the water gets high, the people grab their beer and cards and go to the highest level under the roof and play poker and drink until the water goes down."

Pittsburgh was looking for a story of evacuations and other color and perhaps heroics of rescuing people. Ohioans were accustomed to high water every spring and knew how to deal with it. I knew that. After all, I grew up in that area on the West Virginia side of the river.

Just as every three years when the United Mine Workers Union contract with the coal companies expired and miners were on strike, miners' families knew this was a triennial occurrence and set money aside for their own strike fund. My flood story never saw the light of day outside of Ohio.

Chapter 33

Sandi
Summer 1973
I Meet Red

The night of Major League Baseball's All-Star game in 1973, John had me working night broadcast. The game is always on a Tuesday night. No other baseball is scheduled during that three-day break since Triple-A teams play their All-Star game the next night. I didn't find much other activity in Ohio.

I was working with Jay Gibian, and even that didn't make a quiet night exciting or entertaining. He was working the night news desk and would get all his work done at the start of his shift. Then he leaned back, folded his hands over his stomach, and began twiddling his thumbs! Really! He wasn't that good at finding stories.

Even the teletype operator kept to himself, working on the teletypesetter on the other side of the room.

I had seven broadcast reports to prepare that night and do my own punching on the teletype machine. I was busy. I didn't have much news to work with, and what I did have became staler by the hour. Midway through the night I made a call to the Ohio Highway Patrol's Communications Center to see if anything was happening in Ohio that I could write a couple of sentences about for the broadcast wire.

What I got was a different person, someone I had never spoken with before.

"You're new here," I said.

"I'm filling in for the regular crew, who are attending a retirement party," I was told.

"Oh my gosh." I suddenly remembered. "They told me about that, but I forgot."

I had become phone friends with the men at the Comm Center and spoke freely with them. I spoke with this substitute as I did with the regulars.

"Since we both get off at eleven, why don't we meet for coffee afterward?" I suggested.

He asked for a rain check, saying he had to fly the next day. He worked in the Patrol's aviation division and was just getting back to work after back surgery in the spring.

I didn't think anything more about the conversation. The next afternoon I got a call from this officer, asking if he could cash in the rain check.

I was in no way prepared to go out or meet anyone. We women were not wearing slacks to work, but I had dressed down. I was wearing a sleeveless dress, dirty-white sandals, and no pantyhose. My legs needed a shave.

Do I choose dinner at seven or an after-work drink? I chose the late-night meeting. I found a six-foot gentleman with wavy red hair, standing beside a red car. He was wearing a shirt, tie, and red sport coat. He had told me his name was Red, and I assumed it was because of his red hair. Red was his favorite color too.

We not only struck up a friendship, but also began dating and soon were making plans to be wed. Red and I were married in April 1974, and not only did I become his wife, but also mistress to the two toy poodles he was raising.

As the big day approached, people were asking me if I would keep my name or take his. I was well-known under my maiden name and thought about keeping it, at least in a professional sense. That changed the first time I answered the phone after I returned to work. I answered with Sandi Latimer.

Chapter 34

John

Early 1973
Not a Very Good Year

Just as Sandi's love life was coming together, mine was falling apart. I had been drinking more. I guess I was mimicking those old movies where the journalists drank. Real life wasn't as glamorous as in the movies. I already had the girl but didn't have a good hold on her. She didn't like the drinking.

Joyce and I split in 1973. We began divorce proceedings, and our marriage officially ended the following February.

Not long after the divorce became final, I was visiting with my brother Dave, who is three years younger than I am.

"Did you know Patti's a free woman again?" he asked.

Patti was my high school sweetheart, the girl I had dated in high school but didn't keep in touch with when I went into the air force.

My mind went back to those days. We were at the roller skating rink. I was a junior in high school. This little freshman girl came up to me and asked if I would skate with her. That was the start of my high school romance, which dwindled a couple of years later.

My drinking really started when I was in high school. My classmates were from nearly every European ethnic group: Polish, Italian, Slovenian, Croatian, Greek, and German. Just about every household made its own wine. That wine was Dago Red, which was just about everybody's first drunk.

I also had several friends whose parents owned bars and restaurants, so alcohol was readily available. We had many half-drunk teenagers running around.

"Why do you and your brothers drink when your father and I don't?" Mom would often ask me.

Thanks to my great uncle on Mom's side, I learned about an Irish grandfather on Dad's side who owned a saloon in McMechen, West Virginia, along the Ohio River. He was also a union organizer for the railroad.

Patti's mother's family came from Yugoslavia and her father's family from Lithuania. Patti's father kept a bottle of whisky in the stand at the end of their sofa.

One night when I took Patti home, he said, "Hey, Kady, would you like a drink?"

"Sure," I said. He gave me a glass of whisky and I drank it all—straight.

By the time I got to Okinawa, I was eighteen and starting to get stirred up. Here I was, away from family and my coworkers, away from supervision. Both liquor and women were inexpensive. Prostitution was legal. Sake was a dollar a quart—that's cheap. Young girls were shouting, "Two forty yen and party!" Two forty yen was equivalent to two dollars.

In later years, as Patti and I talked about my days in the air force, Patti was rather blunt about it.

"All you did in Okinawa was drink and shack up with women?" she asked.

That wasn't all I did, but it was a lot of what I did.

After my discharge from the air force, Patti was about to marry another man, although I tried to tell her it was wrong.

I started college and married Joyce. I was twenty-four when we were married. I didn't do that much drinking in college because I didn't have the money, and besides, I had a wife and daughter to support. When I graduated from college, we had one child and I was to start my journalism career two days later. In another year, Gretchen was born.

Along the way, I had heard about and seen many journalists who drank, and I joined that fraternity.

When I worked nights at UPI Charleston, I joined another staffer and a teletype operator for a few drinks after work. I would polish off a pint of whisky and hit some after-hours joints.

By the early 1970s, I was drinking too much. That's probably what led Joyce to ask me to leave her and the girls. They were in their teens and still in school.

Joyce kept the house and I moved out. I spent some time in a motel, and then moved into an apartment in trendy German Village on the south edge of downtown Columbus.

After my divorce became final, when Dave told me that Patti, my high-school sweetheart, was a free woman again, I didn't hesitate. I looked her up and we picked up where we left off. I sent her twenty-three roses, one for each year we had been apart. She had two teenaged children—a boy, Dana, and a girl, Melanie—both with her first husband. Her kids were about the age of Jennifer and Gretchen.

Patti had gone into nurse's training and was a licensed practical nurse, working at Reynolds Memorial Hospital in Glendale, West Virginia.

We were married in June 1974 and settled on the west side of Columbus, just a couple of blocks away from where I had lived with Joyce and the girls.

So often through the years, Patti would say, "If you had written me more often, things might have turned out differently."

Chapter 35

John
Spring 1974
A New Era

"The times they are a changin'," wrote Bob Dylan. And that was what was happening at UPI in early 1974.

My drinking was beginning to catch up with me. It had already wrecked my first marriage, and I was determined it wasn't going to interfere with the second one. I opted to leave the management side of UPI and be one of the reporters. I asked to work the day desk, 6:00 a.m. to 3:00 p.m., Tuesday through Saturday. I could write, but I didn't do the management work any longer. That was the job for the bureau manager who was hired to take my place. Now I had regular hours.

Meanwhile, the contract with the Wire Service Guild expired in mid-March, and negotiations broke down. The Guild went on strike. Jay Gibian was head of the local unit, and most of the employees were Guild members and walked off the job.

Since I was once again a reporter, I had rejoined the Guild. When the strike began, I walked out and took my turn on the picket line in front of the building.

Sandi had reluctantly joined the Guild a year or so after she started working for UPI. By the time of the strike, she was so disenchanted that she called and asked if she could return to work. Management advised her she would have to resign her Guild membership.

She came back to work in a day or so and never mentioned the Guild again. I stayed out for the duration of the strike.

Being on strike meant I missed one of the biggest stories in Ohio. On April 4, a tornado roared through Xenia in southwest Ohio, wiping out about half the town and killing thirty-five people.

I missed working a big story and Sandi was so busy preparing for her wedding that neither one of us remembers much about that coverage.

"Red flew over Xenia," Sandi told of how her future husband had seen the devastation from the air. "He said you could see where it cut a path through the town and Central State University right outside the city limits."

The strike ended a few days later with a new contract, and everyone was back working normal shifts. Within days, no one would have known we had gone through a strike and had been on different sides of issues.

Sandi and Red were married in late April, a couple of weeks after the strike ended.

Another change taking place was in technology. Typewriters were being put aside for computers. Jay had picked up on the new technology and was learning about the function of computers in the newsroom.

Columbus was expecting to get its computers in late spring or early summer. At a higher level, talks were being held about moving to a new location. It would take place about the time we were to get the computers. The news staff picked up on moving. They grumbled about the conditions in which they worked. The desks were grimy. Sandi said it had been a long time since she had worn a white long-sleeved blouse or sweater because the desks were so dirty that she was having trouble getting the cuffs and sleeves clean. Chairs were in poor condition. Seat coverings were cracked, and the women complained those seats ruined their pantyhose. Casters were worn unevenly. The floor tiles weren't that clean. The cleaning personnel couldn't be that proficient, especially when people were working.

Reporters wrote their stories on books that contained four sheets of paper, with carbon paper between them. Working with carbon paper was a dirty job. One of the teletypes used two-copy paper, again with carbon between the pages. It was not unusual for the person working the broadcast desk to wash his or her hands after every split, a twenty-minute period that the state bureaus had to file their reports.

At last, management broke the news to the staff—yes, we were moving. The initial plan was to get the computers set up in the new location on the eighteenth floor of the Lincoln Leveque Tower, a block away in downtown Columbus.

Strange things happened when we were cleaning up to move. A stand with several drawers that stood near where sportswriter Gene Caddes worked had a thick, dark wooden top. It was almost black. Someone started cleaning that top. It turned out to be a butcher-block top! With the top polished, the stand was moved to the new office. No one ever worked at that stand, and it stayed clean the rest of my years at UPI.

At the left side of the teletype machine that carried the Scripps-Howard report was a gigantic cardboard box where tape from that machine accumulated. If we needed Scripps copy, we could take the tape and feed it through our machines. That box was emptied every night. When we shut that machine off for the last time, a lot of memories went with it. Those in the office that last day started laughing.

"Remember?" they said, and started laughing again.

They began reminiscing about the day when Larry Snouffer, one of the teletype operators, came in from a stint in the Scripps office and went to that box to get the tape of a transmission. Just as he reached into that big box to grab a handful of tape, up popped another operator, Otie Snider.

"Wh-wh-wh-wh ..." stammered a shocked Larry, who had jumped backward halfway across the room.

Everyone in the room broke out laughing.

"Scared the poop out of him," David Harding recalled years later when a group of us met for dinner and story swapping.

I had hired David in 1973. He was from Lima in northwest Ohio and had gone to Ohio State for his journalism degree. He was about the age of Otie Snyder, Larry Snouffer, and another operator, Bob Cole—in their mid to late twenties.

Technicians spent many hours that June working at the two locations. Computers were delivered to the new location, and rewiring was done to accommodate them. We were to be out of the old office on a Sunday.

Sandi was scheduled to open the new bureau that Sunday morning. She arrived at the new location but discovered the new office wasn't ready for operation. She started her shift at the old office, and by the middle of her shift, she was able to go to the new office.

"Wow! This is neat!" she exclaimed, walking into the new office, which had royal blue carpeting and new desks. "Now I can buy some white long-sleeved blouses."

The introduction of computers with printers beside every terminal meant the elimination of carbon paper and a cleaner working area.

But as always, the best-laid plans didn't come about. The technicians had to move the old teletype machines to the new office when they hit a snag while rewiring.

Computers sat in the back of the office for several weeks. My staff tried to become accustomed to the touch of their keyboards. They could read instruction books.

"But it doesn't mean anything," Sandi would complain. "I can type, so I don't need to sit here and practice on this computer."

It took a few weeks to get the wiring completed and bring the computers online with other bureaus in the company.

"I'd rather have a hands-on demonstration," Sandi said. "What I'm supposed to do and what the book seems to tell me sound like two different operations."

Most of my staff was able to pick up computer use quickly and make a smooth transition from typewriters. As the staff became more adept at the computers, the teletype operators took retirement. We lost a lot of knowledge when that group left.

"I'm sure some of them were around with carrier pigeons," Sandi joked one day. "I'm really going to miss them. I loved my editing classes in college, but what I learned in class was no match for what I learned from these guys."

Most of the staff was young and could make transitions easily. I worried about the older people. Change was hard to accept. Teletype operator Jim Carter worked the third shift. He opted to try to make the move from teletype operator to editorial if he could still work third shift.

I had hopes for him. A few years earlier, Gene Caddes had made the move from teletype operator to news and became the sports editor. He was knowledgeable about sports and was able to make a smooth transition.

Jim also made the transition and became the standard-bearer on third shift. I felt sorry, though, for Ruth Bynum, another of the teletype operators who tried to move to news side. She was good as an operator, but she found the pressures of news side more than she could handle. Ruth ended up taking a disability retirement, but we kept in touch with her for the rest of her life. Former operators mingled with reporters at her funeral.

UPI continued to do the same style of reporting and sending stories to newspaper, radio, and TV clients, many of whom probably never knew what changes were taking place in our office. Perhaps they did, though, since they were probably going through some changes themselves.

A couple of years into our new style of work, Mason Blosser decided to take his retirement. He was a fascinating man: he had a master's in journalism from Medill School of Journalism at Northwestern; he had had polio and had been left with slightly deformed hands but was surprisingly fast at typing. He also had a pilot's license, but in recent years had chosen to spend his free time on a powerboat on Lake Erie, where he and his wife had a mobile home to which they would retire.

The introduction of computers seemed to speed up the number of stories that could be transmitted. We didn't like to see the wires sitting idle between stories. After all, our clients had been brought up that the machines were constantly moving and clacking.

I'm glad my staff was able to adapt to these technological changes. I knew I had hired a competent staff.

Chapter 36

Sandi
Fall 1975
Rosemary Comes to Columbus

In late 1975 John hired another woman, Rosemary Armao. She had come from the Albany, New York, bureau, and was joining her husband in Columbus. He was working at Ohio State University, and they were expecting their first child.

This was something new for me. I was working with a woman, and a pregnant one at that. Other women had worked at UPI during my time, but since I worked night and overnight shifts—second and third shifts—I didn't associate much with them because they worked dayside.

They didn't work very long, either as summer relief or a short time to gain experience and move on. I didn't have much time to get close to them. Moreover, I didn't know if it was kosher to be close friends with coworkers, but with Rosemary, it was different. She and I were assigned to work together quite a bit.

Her baby was due in early July. On a night in late June, the weather was stormy. Tornado warnings had even been issued. I had the night off and was home alone with the dogs. I had let them out but sat on the back steps waiting for them to do their business. I started thinking: *I'd better keep an eye on Rosemary. What if she goes into labor on a night that we are working together? I have to be strong for her. I don't know what to do.*

The next afternoon when I arrived for my night broadcast shift a little before three o'clock, I noticed that those in the office were not the ones who had been on the schedule. *Where is everyone?* I wondered. *Am I in the right room? The right day?*

"Did you hear?" exclaimed our summer help Henry Reske as I was checking the schedule. "Rosemary had her baby last night."

I turned around and looked at him with my mouth wide-open.

"During the tornado warnings?" I asked. "Oh my!"

About two weeks later Rosemary came back to work for a couple of hours a day.

"All I want to do is hold the baby," she said. "I have to get a break, get away from that."

She'd schedule much of her work around the time I was working and we would chat. We began to get closer. Gradually her hours increased until she was back full-time. She worked nights while her husband worked days, and that cut down on the amount of child care they needed.

Not only did we grow closer as coworkers; we also became closer as friends. I think it was good for me. I was developing a friendly relationship with a coworker and one that could continue outside the office. She'd write a feature story. I had the feeling if she could write a feature story, so could I. We relied on each other to edit each other's stories. If I were lost for a word while writing a story I'd holler, "I need a word," and she'd come to my terminal, read my story, and help me find the right word.

I'm glad we were working together so well, especially the night of May 28, 1977. That was Memorial Day weekend, and our leaders were at the King's Island Resort Hotel north of Cincinnati for a long weekend with their families.

I was working the night desk, and Rosemary was on the broadcast shift. At the start of a holiday weekend, not much was going on. I took a phone call from a stringer in Cincinnati.

"There's a fire in a night club across the Ohio River in northern Kentucky," the stringer said. "I can see smoke from the station."

That had to be big if he could see smoke from that far away. I asked him for all the information he could give us. Rosemary was reading over my shoulder as I typed the notes and began making mental notes. She went around to the other side of the back-to-back terminals and got the broadcast *urgents* out and helped make phone calls while I fielded incoming calls. With computers, we could send our copy attention to another bureau ourselves and not have to wait on someone else to do it.

The next call from the first stringer reported: "John Davidson was performing."

Our concern then was, "Is he safe?"

Then calls such as: "Five hundred people in the building."

"Rosemary," I called over the terminals, "we gotta get help. Call Ed. He's at King's Island. He's close. I'll call Rick."

Ed was our state editor, Ed DiPietro. He could help direct coverage since he was about thirty miles north of the fire. Rick was Rick Van Sant, who was bureau manager in Cincinnati. He had been given the position in Cincinnati when he came back from the service. During his time in Vietnam, his then-girlfriend Betty had moved on.

We had a major story on our hands and it was a holiday weekend. This was beginning to sound familiar: a holiday weekend, a major story, and the only people around were those who were scheduled to work.

When notified of a story, reporters have pad, pen, and a roll of coins as handy as car keys, and they are ready to move. Stories have been told about some reporters, especially those in Washington, who had packed bags in the office, in their vehicles, and by the front door at home. Rick was on the story immediately.

Rosemary and I kept the story moving and getting it to New York the best we could through phone calls in and out of Cincinnati until we made contact with Rick on the scene.

As many as five hundred people had crowded into the Beverly Hills Supper Club high on a hill across the Ohio River from Cincinnati. The highly rated restaurant drew big-name entertainers.

Rick was writing in his head as he gathered information and then dictating straight to New York. That meant we could get the story on the wires quicker.

His writing, as always, was sharp and colorful, even when he had been on the scene for long hours.

About the second day into the story, I took a call from a person on the New York general desk who seemed terribly upset.

"We have to get the death count up," he said. "ROX (the terminology we used for our competitor, the Associated Press) has as many as 500 dead and we're going with 165."

"That's what Rick has counted and what he has sent," I said. "I'll get back with him and check again."

It was hard getting hold of him in the mass of media that had gathered for a major story. Cell phones weren't in use yet. I called several Cincinnati radio and TV stations and left word for them to tell Rick to call me.

Soon I got a call from Rick and I relayed the messages from New York.

"They're sounding irate and bugging me," I said.

"There are only 165 white sheets," Rick said of the number of victims lying in a makeshift morgue. "I counted them. Several times."

"That's what I've told New York, but they want the number to match the five hundred that AP is going with."

"I'm not going to make up the numbers," Rick said. "I'll call New York."

AP had been going with "at least five hundred" as the number of victims, and was winning the logs with that. We were going with the lower number, although we had the better written story.

When the final count was made known, it was 165 dead and many injured. We were right all along and lost the logs to AP, which had such nebulous numbers and had to backtrack.

"It's easier to raise the death toll than it is to play God and resurrect victims," I said again.

I had first said that not long after I started working for UPI.

One night, Bill Clark, news director of WKBN in Youngstown, called to tell me of an explosion—two people dead and an unknown number of injuries. I asked what hospitals the dead and injured were taken to. I called around Youngstown and found one body. I kept going with one dead, even though Bill, a trusted newsman, kept after me saying, "I said two were dead."

I argued politely, "Bill, I can only find one body. When I find the second body, I'll up it to two dead."

The next day he called back, all apologetic.

"Sandi, you were right. There was only one dead," he said, and apologized for the way he treated me.

I often wondered how long it took him to remember that conversation and call me.

Chapter 37

Sandi

January 1978
Too Windy, Too Cold, Too Snowy

On a cold evening in late January 1978, I was working night broadcast. Something had happened outside but I didn't know what. I had heard that it would rain. Rain is unusual in late January. Suddenly the weather wire started updating the forecasts. I hadn't any more than sent out the evening forecasts on the 5:30 p.m. split before they were updated. I had to type them again. The weather was getting bad. I couldn't see much out of the window of the eighteenth floor of a downtown office building that late at night. Weather statistics kept showing a falling barometric pressure. Something was wrong, but I couldn't figure it out. I didn't know that much about what a falling barometric pressure meant. I only knew I had never experienced anything like this since I had started working in news.

At the end of my shift, I drove home in a cold rain, almost sleet, all on top of the many inches of snow we already had. The wind was strong, and I could hear it howling when I got into the house. I let my two toy poodles out, but they didn't want to stay out long. When they came in, I went out to retrieve the red ceramic fireplug my mother had made the dogs for Christmas. I feared the strong wind would break it, and Mom had put too much hard work into it to have it destroyed so soon.

My husband, who had retired from the Highway Patrol, was working in security at Bank Ohio. He was on the third shift at the bank's new headquarters building downtown. I was alone with two small dogs.

About the time I would normally get up in the morning, Red called. That's when I discovered we were without power. Red told me to stay in bed, where it was warm. Power out was in many places. He said he was going to work overtime because the morning shift couldn't make it in. In fact, he didn't think many people would.

He had my curiosity aroused. I got up and let the dogs out. I was surprised at what I saw. While I slept the wind continued, and the sleet changed to snow as the temperatures dropped. The wind had created deep snowdrifts. Within minutes my power returned. I started to do my regular housework, but the power went off when I tried to turn on the dryer to finish laundry I had started the day before. So much for that. No wonder Red said stay in bed.

It wasn't long before John called to see what my situation was.

"Power is off and on," I told him. "Red's working late because his replacement folks can't get in. I'm here with the two dogs."

John was an animal lover himself. He told me that Ohio was pretty much closed. A blizzard had shut down almost everything. For those who did make it to work, he made reservations for two rooms at one of the downtown hotels where they could stay if they couldn't get home. He told me not to worry about getting to work.

I summoned enough courage to turn on the TV for the noon news, hoping my power wouldn't go out again. The station I was watching had sent a news truck to a big truck stop in the county west of us. People were stranded. The news crew was stranded out there as well that day.

Red called a couple of times to keep me apprised of his situation and to find out how I was doing. I didn't keep the radio or TV on very long for fear I would lose power. It would go off for a few minutes and then come back on. I had the drapes open to rely on natural daylight, or as much as I could get through the frosted-over windows. I passed time with a good book, and the two dogs curled up with me under a blanket.

"Is this how I'm spending the day when we're having the biggest story of the year?" I moaned to the dogs as I walked around the house, knowing that I should be doing something but not knowing what.

On one call, Red said he was going to work all night again. No one could get anywhere. By morning, things were better, and he called to say he was heading home. He would leave a little after seven o'clock. I knew it would take him longer than usual because of the road conditions. We still had high snowdrifts. Road crews were working the best they could, but the temperatures were low. Freeways were cleared first, then state highways, and down the line of major arteries and finally side streets. It was hard telling when crews would get to the major streets, let alone the side streets.

Finally the doorbell rang and there was pounding on the door. Red was hollering for me to help open the door. I tried, but the storm doors were frozen shut. Since I couldn't put the dogs out, I was constantly cleaning up after them in the basement. I managed to hear Red tell me that his car, a 1977 red Ford LTD, had stranded him—the fuel line had frozen. He had to walk a short distance. Thank heaven he was wearing his snowmobile suit. Both of us pounding on the door frame freed the ice, and he was able to get inside. He looked like the Abominable Snowman.

He got some sleep but had to go back to work that night. Someone from the bank had a four-wheel-drive vehicle and came out to get him. That was my day off, and I wanted to go to the office and help out. Those two days had to be the worst days I spent. I wanted to work but couldn't get there.

Had that happened a generation later, I could have made some phone calls from home and fed information via the computer. But in the late seventies, computers were in their infancy, and telecommuting, e-mail, and blogs were unheard of. Even the Radio Shack TRS-80 that reporters would use at the scene and file stories with over telephone wires were several years from becoming commonplace in our newsroom.

What had happened that night was a blizzard, and it hit the entire state of Ohio. It took a couple of days to get roads open and life back to normal—or as normal as we could get. The snow hung around for a long time, but once the roads were cleared, Ohio went back to work.

Throughout the ordeal, we were without power at home for only six hours. Other people were not as fortunate. They were out for more than twenty-four hours. This was the first blizzard I knew about, but not the first one I'd been through.

I had gone to college in northeast Ohio. In January of my sophomore year, we had a lot of snow and strong winds on Sunday night. Classes were canceled Monday. Snowfall totaled thirteen inches. It was up to my knees. Since I didn't have classes, I thought I'd head to the library to get working on an assignment. At that time, in the early 1960s, we women were not allowed to wear slacks in campus buildings. I dressed the best I could, in layers, from head to toe. Snow fell into my boots, which were nearly knee-high. I trudged across campus only to find the library closed. I couldn't get a cup of coffee because the Student Union was also closed. Back to my residence hall I went. Road crews had worked long hours to clear the roads, and classes were back in session the next day. We just thought it was a snowstorm. Years later I heard it was a blizzard.

Chapter 38

John
January 1978
Blizzard Conditions

I had been in touch with the crew throughout the evening and managed to get to work in the middle of the night. The rain was beginning to change to snow, and the wind was blowing strong. Once again, as bureau manager, I would be working the main desk. I made calls to the Highway Patrol posts, sheriffs' offices, police departments, hospitals, and our client newspapers.

We had a light brown recipe box on the desk that held file cards with phone numbers in every city and county in the state. I had used that so much over the years that I knew some of the numbers without looking them up. Those cards had been handled so much that they were gray and dog-eared.

By daybreak when people were waking up, they found themselves snowbound. I didn't have many people at work that day because they couldn't get in. All activities were canceled.

The main story that day was the weather. I made phone calls and typed my notes into the computer system as I was talking to people. We didn't get any more than a good chunk of copy written before we had a power outage and lost everything. That's when we learned to save the copy after almost every paragraph. I came to know what they mean when they say to save often.

As I made my calls, I had some good quotes from people. I still remember a quote from one family in Darke County in western Ohio along the Indiana border: "We have three blankets and faith in God," they told me.

I worked until seven o'clock that night and managed to get a motel room in German Village on the south side of downtown. I drove down on the main street—High Street, US 23. The next morning a cabdriver helped me start my car so I could drive to the Statehouse Underground Parking Garage. Not long after I started out, I ran into a pile of snow. Luckily a police cruiser was close by. It had a big wooden board for a bumper and the officer pushed me up High Street.

The following day my regular crew started dragging in at their scheduled hours. We didn't have much of a dress code to start with, and on this occasion, everyone was wearing blue jeans and flannel shirts and sweaters—anything to keep warm and dry.

The focal point of the storm moved to the Statehouse and the office of Governor James A. Rhodes. Whoever was available went to the governor's media briefings. Slowly Ohio returned to normal.

At the time, the Palace Theatre on the ground level of our building was being renovated. The marquee had a four-word phrase on it: "Closed until further notice." Our photographer Terry Bochatey had taken a photo of the marquee and transmitted it to clients. The phrase really summed up Ohio those first couple of days.

Chapter 39

Sandi

Summer 1979
Women in Sports

Gene Caddes had started his UPI career as a teletype operator, but when a sports writing position opened, he opted to move to the writing side.

He was knowledgeable about sports, and did we have the sports! Tops, of course, was Ohio State University. Football was king and basketball had fallen somewhat. We usually had a big golf tournament close by. High school sports always played a big role. Cincinnati and Cleveland sports were handled by writers in those cities.

Gene feared his writing wasn't that good. I'd take dictation from him, and he'd always tell me to make sure it sounded good. I was knowledgeable about both sports and writing, and he knew I wouldn't let anything go out that wasn't right.

He was good at covering such events, interviewing the participants, and writing stories. Feature writing was something he'd pass on. A couple of the more unusual ideas for stories I wrote came from Gene.

One morning he found a thick manila envelope on his desk. Looking through it, he decided it wasn't anything he could tackle, so he put it in my mailbox. In my spare time that evening I went through the package and tried to figure out what it meant. The next morning from home I called the ad agency where the person worked who had left the package for Gene.

"I'd like to speak to Lee," and I began to stumble over the last name, which started with the letter D and looked like it was French.

"Oh, you want to talk to Lee Durieux," the receptionist at the ad agency said. She pronounced it Duryea, like the name of an automotive pioneer.

I spoke with Lee for a few minutes and agreed to meet him the next day. We went to lunch at the dining room of a hotel a block from his office. That was about four blocks from our office. He explained that he had written an outdoor musical drama that was presented each summer in an amphitheater on the southern Ohio land of sausage king Bob Evans, who was one of his clients. Each year he tried to add a new scene to the drama to encourage people to make a return visit. This year's new scene pertained to the battle for the strip of land between Detroit and Toledo in the 1830s. Although the battle was waged in Congress, Lee had used a game between Indians and settlers that was to resemble a football game between well-known college football rivals Ohio State and Michigan. One side was to be dressed in scarlet and gray and the other side in maize and blue.

After lunch, Lee and I went to the boiler room of the hotel where the upright piano was stored at that time, and we played songs from the Charlie Brown Christmas movie. He wanted to show me that one of the songs he had incorporated into the drama was similar to one from the Charlie Brown program.

My husband and I attended a presentation of the drama that summer. Prior to the show we had eaten at a barbecue and enjoyed mint juleps on Bob Evans's lawn.

After I wrote the story, Gene complimented me: "I could never have done a story like that."

Lee and I remained friends until his death a few years later. He introduced me to a woman who worked in public relations at the Bob Evans corporate office, and another longtime friendship resulted. The two of us attended Lee's funeral.

Lee also steered me to one of his coworkers who offered me some stories that got good play for me—and provided another longtime friendship.

A second story idea Gene shared meant a lot to me.

"Why don't you interview wives of athletes and coaches and find out how they survive the season?" he suggested in late spring of 1979. "I'll get you names and phone numbers."

He, John, and I talked it over, and I received the go-ahead to do the story. Gene produced names and numbers of several people—Jean Bruce, wife of the OSU football coach, Earle Bruce; Sondra Burson, wife of the Muskingum College basketball coach, Jim Burson, and mother of high school standout Jay Burson; Marlene Faust, wife of Gerry Faust, an outstanding high school coach at Cincinnati Moeller; wives of Cincinnati Bengals players Archie Griffin and Kenny Anderson; and wives of the Cincinnati Reds manager, John McNamara, and Cleveland Indians manager, Jeff Torborg; as well as other athletes at all levels in Ohio.

I made phone calls and conducted interviews. I worked with photographers in Columbus, Cleveland, and Cincinnati to get photos to go with the story. I sorted through notes, organized notes, and wrote and wrote and wrote. I had stories on three different angles. I reread the stories, edited, and had a couple of other people in the office read and edit the stories, which were going to run as a three-part series.

We notified the New York sports desk what was in the works, and the men were excited about this. We had decided that we would send it to New York Sports around noon on a Monday. The stories would run on the sports wire for release on Tuesday, Wednesday, and Thursday. We would then run the story on the newspaper wire for the newspapers that didn't have the sports wire.

At the time I wrote the stories, Jeff Torborg was on the hot seat with the Cleveland Indians, who as usual, were not doing well. I had had a long interview with his wife, Suzie. I worked a second shift Sunday and didn't get up until around nine o'clock Monday. The first thing I heard when I turned on the radio was that the Indians had fired Jeff Torborg.

"Oh my God," I said, drawing out each word. I dressed in record time, put my pet dogs in the basement, and headed downtown. I ran from the parking lot to the building where our offices were on the eighteenth floor. I don't think I spoke to anyone in the office as I raced to a vacant seat and a phone near a computer and punched in the number of the Cleveland Indians.

"I wrote a story after an interview with Suzie Torborg, and the story is to move this afternoon," I told the Indians' public information officer after I identified myself. "Now that Jeff has been fired, I need to speak to Suzie again to freshen the story. Can you put me in touch with her?" I begged.

My heart was pounding. I kept taking deep breaths.

"Just a minute," the PR rep told me. A minute later, Suzie was on the phone. We chatted for a while, and after wishing her good luck, I hung up and started writing my stories again. I rewrote the stories and sent them to New York on time.

I leaned back and let my arms dangle as I breathed a sigh of relief. It was done. Finally! Now to sit back and see how many newspapers used the story.

The three stories came back immediately on the sports wire as I sent them. That afternoon we moved the first one on the Ohio wire with an advisory that this was the first of a three-part series and that the other two would move Tuesday and Wednesday. These would be for release Tuesday, Wednesday, and Thursday.

Baseball was the main sport at that time, and not much else was happening. College football had not yet started summer practices. The NBA and NHL seasons were over, and NFL teams were about to get started at training camps. It seemed such a good time to send this type of series.

I could hardly wait to go through the Tuesday newspapers when the mail arrived Wednesday. I sorted out the papers, pulling out the Tuesday editions and stacking them beside my workstation so I could go through them throughout the evening to see who used the story. I was getting good play. Almost every paper I saw was using it. I was pleased.

I was working the main desk that night. It was unusual that the New York Yankees would have the night off.

In the middle of the evening, a gentleman from Akron who

monitored the police scanner called. He usually had some piddly information that I really didn't need, but I'd thank him anyway.

"Thurman Munson's plane just crashed," he said. "Thurman Munson was doing touch-and-go's (landings and immediate takeoffs) at the Akron-Canton Airport."

I thanked him profusely and composed an urgent message to our Cleveland office and the New York sports desk, tipping them off.

Thurman Munson, a native of Canton and a graduate of Kent State University, was the All-Star catcher of the New York Yankees. He was flying a twin-engine Cessna Citation and practicing takeoffs and landings at the Akron-Canton Airport that night. He crashed on one of the landings and the plane burst into flames, killing him.

John Spetz in the Cleveland office worked to get information on the crash, while the New York sports desk pulled together background information on Munson and sent the obituary for the news wire. It helped tremendously to have an obituary prepared and sitting in a hold file to be used when necessary.

I had taken a moment to call John to advise him of what had happened.

"There goes the third part of my series," I cried into the phone. "Nobody is going to use the third part tomorrow. They won't have room."

"Don't worry," John said, trying to allay my fears. "They'll use it. They've used the first two. They can't drop it. If they don't use it tomorrow, they'll use it Friday."

I couldn't see using the final part on Friday. Friday was the start of a new month, and one of the newspapers we had was terminating our service at the end of the month and going with AP. That paper would have to use the story Thursday.

I took a deep breath and went about my work. The next day I checked the Wednesday papers, and again many papers used my second part. Friday, I was afraid to look at Thursday papers. I did so with a lot of skepticism and emotion. Sports pages carried two main stories— the Thurman Munson plane crash and my third part of the series. I breathed a sigh of relief.

I had my tear sheets and pride for a story well done. That fall I attended a meeting of the Ohio Newspaper Women's Association. A woman from the *Cambridge Jeffersonian* came up to me, introduced herself, and thanked me for the series.

"I hope you don't mind that I used your idea and wrote stories on our local wives," she said.

"No, I don't mind," I said. I really didn't mind. After all, I had it first. Thank you, Gene, for the idea.

Later in the NFL season, wives of players would be interviewed at halftime of the games.

"They stole your story," my husband would say.

I smiled. It's nice to be imitated.

Chapter 40

Sandi

Summer 1981
Parents of Pregnant Teens Talk

Not only did story ideas come from my fellow workers, but they also came from clients and stringers. One idea came from Jodi Gossage, a stringer and a student in a journalism class at Ohio State that my friend and coworker Rosemary was teaching one fall quarter. Jodi would pop in the office occasionally, write a story, and chat with us before heading home to her daughter.

One day she suggested that we do a story together. Her idea was a story on parents' reactions to their pregnant teenagers. She suggested going to the east side of Columbus and talking to parents of teenage mothers.

I nixed that idea. I didn't think that a portion of a large city would produce a good enough sampling. It would have to be all throughout the city and include all parts of the socioeconomic scale. I wasn't sure how to go about that.

"It's a nonstory in just one part of the city," I told John a day or so later when we were talking about it.

I really didn't want to do the story with a stringer. I'm not vain, but I have to be honest: I wanted the glory to myself. In many cases, stringers didn't hang around too long, and Jodi was only doing it for the one quarter she had the class.

I didn't give up on the idea. The suggestion was pushed to the back of my mind. It wouldn't go away.

A month or so later, I was reading a story in a newspaper about an obstetrician in Marion, about an hour north of Columbus, who had helped create a program to help teenage mothers deal with their children, return to school, and hopefully not have another teen or unwed pregnancy.

The program was created after the obstetrician and a pediatrician argued over whose patient that teenage girl in labor was. Their research of similar cases led them to become concerned about the high number of teenage pregnancies. The year before, the rural county had little more than a thousand births, and 250 of them were to women under the age of twenty—one fourth of all the births were to teenagers!

I thought about the connection. It sounded like what I wanted, but then again, it didn't. This program dealt with teenagers, not their parents. I developed a list of questions and how I wanted to pursue the story. I called the doctor and explained what I wanted. He was receptive to my idea but said he would have to look for parents who would be willing to be interviewed. I started talking with John about what I was planning. I didn't think he seemed too excited. Then I went in to talk with Ed DiPietro, our state editor.

"We've done stories on pregnant teenagers," he said.

"I'm not talking about the pregnant teenagers," I countered. "I'm talking about interviewing their parents."

"We don't need it," he maintained.

I didn't think he was paying attention to me. I was determined I was going to do the story. I sat down with Rosemary and talked about it.

"Go for it," she said.

"Will you help me?" I asked.

"You don't have to ask," she said. "I'll help in any way I can."

I knew I could count on her. We had become close friends in the few years since she came to Columbus from Albany, New York. I wrote features, and she concentrated on in-depth stories.

About a month after the initial contact with the obstetrician, I called back to see what he had accomplished.

"When are you coming up?" he asked.

I spent my days off the next couple of weeks in late winter of 1981 in Marion, where the doctor had set me up with parents. We talked at roundtable discussions, one-on-one interviews, with the doctor, and even over dinner with the parents of a boy.

Parents talked, cried, wiped tears, and talked some more. One of the more poignant statements came from a woman who said she took her daughter to a clinic to "abort my first grandchild."

I had tapes and a notebook full of notes. I had good quotes, but one thing I had to overcome—the people didn't want their real names used. I told them if that was the way they felt, I could give them different names and add an editor's note to the top of the story that real names were not used at the request of those interviewed. I had never encountered anything like that before.

I had a lot to digest. How was I going to write it? I couldn't go to John and I couldn't go to Ed. They didn't seem that strongly in favor of this story. I talked to Rosemary and I called the features desk in New York. I was becoming friends with the reporters who worked in that department. They liked my ideas for stories and were excited about this one. They told me if I became stuck, they'd help me.

I started writing. This was not going to be a four hundred- or five-hundred-word story like most of my features were. This one kept growing. It was destined to be a Sunday Lifestyle piece.

I let the story sit for a while after I wrote it. Then I asked Rosemary to read and edit it. This story took up five takes in a hold file that would keep it longer than the forty-eight hours before purging as the active files did. I had to keep each take to less than one thousand words because that was the maximum a file would hold. My story was running around forty-five hundred words. I sent it to the New York features desk. The reporters read it and told me it was good. This story was put on the schedule to run early in the week so newspapers that had Sunday editions could make plans for its use.

I told John and Ed that it would be running and would be for weekend release.

The day it was scheduled to move on the A wire, the prime wire where all major stories were carried, I was on hand to see what New York had done to the story. They had done nothing other than precede it with an advisory that a lengthy weekend feature would follow in five takes.

"It's moving!" I shouted. I was excited. I'd never had such a story before.

Ed came out of his office to see what the excitement was about. When he noticed the advisory and my story, he sat down at the computer and typed out an advisory to Ohio editors that a five-part series would be moving on the Ohio newspaper wire.

"It's in five takes, not a five-part series," I said. He didn't listen. He sent out the advisory that a five-part series would soon be moving.

A five-part series is one thing; a story in five takes is another. A five-part series means five different stories and each can stand on its own. A story in five takes means it is a long story and has been broken into five pages to make it more manageable for editors to handle.

Again I was hurt after trying to talk to him. I was getting nowhere with him. I didn't know where to turn, and I was getting mad.

"He's screwing me," I said as I walked over to the table by the door where the newspapers were spread out when the mail was brought up. "No one is going to use it."

I was sorting through papers when I heard bells. I went over to the bank of printers to see what was coming across. It was the A wire, and a bulletin had broken into my feature story.

A bulletin carries five bells. It will break into the story that is moving, put the word "more" at the end of the current paragraph, then pick up the original story after the bulletined item moves. That's the way it appeared on hard copy. The computerized item was intact.

The bulletined story was about a Pulitzer Prize winner from the *Washington Post* having to forfeit her coveted award. Janet Cooke had won the prize for her well-written feature story on drug use in the nation's capital that focused on an eight-year-old child.

Within days of the announcement of the awards, Cooke and her story began to unravel. When a newspaper started checking her résumé, she broke down, admitting the résumé was a fake, that she had not graduated from the University of Toledo, and that the little boy she profiled did not exist.

All that came out when my story was moving where I had given the people I interviewed different names. I had promised them anonymity, the first—and only—time I ever did that. They wouldn't have talked to me if I had insisted on using their real names.

A little later when Rosemary came in, I was a basket case. I was just short of tears.

"What's wrong?" she asked as I joined her in the back area where she had gone to pour herself a cup of coffee.

We stood beside the coat closet. She reached over to put her hands over mine as I explained what had happened with Janet Cooke and how I felt it could affect my story.

"It's a good story and papers are going to use it," she said, hugging me. "Those Ohio editors are smart enough to see the story for what it's worth. And don't let that Janet Cooke mess bother you. She made up a character for her story; you interviewed people."

I had already called the New York features desk to talk with them about the Janet Cooke Pulitzer Prize situation. They assured me, God love 'em, that I was fine.

I had called the doctor to let him know that the story would be moving on a certain day and would be for release the following weekend. It was too bad the newspaper in Marion wouldn't have the story. It was an AP-serviced paper. I'd have to get copies of newspapers that used the story and send him a copy.

This was the second time I had an enterprising story and something happened to cause me to worry about its usage. I came through the first time. Would I come through this time? I had to sit back and wait.

I didn't have to wait long. The *Columbus Citizen-Journal* used the story the next morning, or at least the first take. The story had an editor's advisory about a five-part series and only the first take was used. In that take, I started with identifying several of the people and their situation, setting the stage for what was to come. The last paragraph of that take said, "They found a friend in a Marion obstetrician." I started the second take with naming the doctor and told what he had done. The newspaper never used the rest of the story. I felt cheated, and I also felt local readers were being cheated.

By Sunday afternoon and Monday, I began to get messages from people in our bureaus around the country telling me newspapers in their area used the story. I perked up.

A week or so later when a package came in the mail from the New York headquarters, a couple of envelopes were for me. One large one had tear sheets of my story from newspapers around the country.

The other was a manila-colored, business-sized envelope used for interoffice mail. Inside that was a regular business envelope from the New York office addressed to me. It was from the editor-in-chief, H. L. Stevenson, complimenting me on my enterprising story.

I read it several times and went around showing it to everyone.

"He doesn't do that often," John said.

Ed looked at it and handed it back to me without comment. I think he was still miffed at me, and I know I was miffed at the way he acted when I tried to talk with him about the story.

Hal, our salesperson, was in the office that day, and I showed the letter to him.

"You should have had photos with that story," he said.

"I had enough trouble getting these people to talk with me," I said. "I had to promise them I wouldn't use their real names. I didn't like to do that."

"At least you could have had a headshot of the doctor," he said. He sounded cold to me about the story.

"Where were you when I was talking about doing it?" I said as I turned around and walked out of his office.

I never could figure out why the men in my office were so cool toward me and this story. Only Rosemary and the people at the New York features desk were helpful.

Chapter 41

Sandi

Spring 1982
Teacher of the Year

I often said the most exciting part of my job was answering phones. I never knew who or what was on the other end.

One call early in 1982 stands out. On the other end of the line was Jim Croneis, publisher of the *Bucyrus Telegraph-Forum*, one of our client newspapers and one we were working hard to keep from going to our opposition.

I'd known Jim for years. He delivered the paper there when I was an area correspondent in high school. He worked his way up the ranks. He also knew my parents when they ran a restaurant.

"You know Wally Brombacher?" Jim asked that morning on the phone.

"Sure do," I said. "What's up with him?"

Wally had worked for the Bucyrus post office for years. I met him when he'd stop in the family restaurant when I was in high school. I met his wife through the Little Theatre not long after I graduated from college.

"He's strutting around town so proud his buttons are about to pop," Jim said.

"Why?" I asked.

"His son Bruce is the Ohio Teacher of the Year and in the running for national Teacher of the Year," Jim said. "They're all going to Washington in March. Bruce teaches down there by you, and I'd like to have a story on him."

"No problem," I said. "I'll get you one."

That was another service we provided to our subscribers. I could easily slip out to the school where Bruce taught, sit through his classes, interview him and his fellow teachers and administrators, write the story, and have it ready when we needed it.

I tapped on John's office door and poked my head in. "Got a minute?"

"What's on your mind?" he said as I plopped in a chair, stretched out my legs, and dropped my arms alongside the chair—my way of relaxing.

After telling him of Jim's request, I said, "I can slip out to Jones Middle School and spend time with Bruce."

"Go for it," he said. "I'll give you a feature day."

That was a perk for doing feature stories. I had one of those days every other week or so. I could do anything I wanted. If I didn't want to come to work, I didn't have to, but I never reached that point. I didn't want to abuse my gift. Sometimes I would schedule an interview, then go into the office, write the story, and go home.

Often I would do interviews by phone and work on the feature story between pieces of my regular work, whether I was working on the main desk or on the broadcast desk. If I were working the third shift, I could do the interviews during the day and write the story in a slow period in the middle of the night.

I was the only one who had feature days. No one complained—or at least I never heard it if they did. And I produced stories. No one else wanted to write feature stories. They didn't think they had the flair for it that I did.

I called the Jones Middle School in the Columbus suburb of Upper Arlington where Bruce taught and explained that I was assigned to do a story on him as the selection for the National Teacher of the Year approached.

I sat through his science classes one afternoon, then spent time with him after the school day. At the start of the interview, I introduced myself as being from the same town as he was, but that I was a few years ahead of him and I knew his parents. He recognized my maiden name, and as he was trying to figure out where he had heard it, I realized that my brother, who spent his senior year at the school Bruce attended, was in his class.

"That's where I heard that name," he said.

I wrote the story and put it in a hold file in the computer system. An abstract I printed off had the notation on it not to move the story until the National Teacher of the Year was announced in Washington. Had he not won the top honor, I could have rewritten a paragraph to reflect that he was one of the finalists.

That day arrived, and I was working on features when the announcement was made. True to the tip, Bruce Brombacher was named the National Teacher of the Year. Immediately after the national story moved, we followed with our Ohio sidebar on Bruce.

The story hadn't any more than cleared the wire than we got a call from Jim Croneis thanking us for our good work.

A satisfied client—that's what we liked to have.

A couple of weeks later, John told me he'd had a phone call from Jim Croneis. John said Jim had told him his counterpart at the Associated Press went to Bucyrus in an attempt to woo the paper to its side. He showed a story the AP had done on Bruce Brombacher as National Teacher of the Year. The story on Bruce ran about a week or so after the fact. Jim pulled out the paper from the day of the announcement that had both the national story and the state sidebar I wrote.

I can still picture that AP man walking out of the building with a frown, saying, "Curses. Foiled again."

Or maybe something a little stronger.

Chapter 42

Sandi

June 2, 1982
A Dollar Goes a Long Way

I'm not much of a betting person, but if I were, I'd lay odds that not many employees chat about the founding of their company. In fact, how many even know about the founding and its early days?

Quite often at UPI we'd mention the names of our founders—E. W. Scripps and Roy Howard—who created United Press in 1907 as a competitor to the Associated Press, which had been in operation for several years.

AP was founded as a cooperative, with its member papers contributing stories. Scripps thought the structure of AP was a big trust, so he and fellow journalist Howard brought Publisher's Press together with Scripps-McRae Press Association and Scripps News Association to form a business known as United Press.

In 1958, after three years of negotiations, William Randolph Hearst's International News Service merged with UP to form UPI.

"The doors of INS were padlocked when INS employees came to work," Ted Virostko would often say of the day of the merger.

He had worked for INS and was one of the few fortunate reporters to be brought over to the new company. In later years, Ted left UPI for Scripps-Howard, a small wire service that provided news to its newspapers and shared them with UPI. In Columbus, Scripps-Howard was next door to UPI.

The merger also brought along the slogan "Get it first, but first get it right." That slogan has often been considered a mantra for many news organizations, but it originated at INS. It also adorned the wall of the student newspaper office at Kent State.

We journalists knew our history because we had studied it in our classes in college.

The wire services began by serving newspapers, but in the 1920s when radio was developed and news became a staple, AP and UPI began broadcast writing. UPI was in the lead in developing a package of stories on the broadcast wire that radio stations could use for their newscasts. Not only did AP and UPI go head-to-head in news stories, but also in the ways the stories were written and packaged.

In the early days, copy was transmitted in Morse code. Technological improvements were slow in those days. Eventually teletypes came into use. Holes that operators punched into tape meant letters and somewhat resembled Morse code.

I think most of the operators in the UPI office when I started were about as old as the company. They'd often entertain us with stories of the old days.

One of my favorite operators was Dick O'Connell. He was an outdoors person and owned a cabin in the Canadian wilderness. It was not unusual for him to invite another UPI employee to join him on a week's vacation that included some fishing.

He'd start telling stories of the old days, and I often wondered if he knew Martha, the last carrier pigeon.

Dick and I shared a love of antique clocks, but he collected them—I only admired them. They lined a shelf that he installed throughout the house he shared with his wife.

Dick helped me learn to read tape. I can still picture the configurations of dots on tape today and think I could pick out a few letters.

As technology improved and computers became the lifestyle, we bid adieu to the operators and moved into a new era.

In 1982, as UPI approached its seventy-fifth anniversary, it had two thousand employees in 224 news and picture bureaus and served more than 7,500 newspapers and radio, television, and cable systems in one hundred countries. In 1958, at the time of the UP merger with INS to become UPI, the company had six thousand employees and served five thousand newspapers and radio stations. Talk about doing more with less!

Meanwhile, everyone faced economic issues. Inflation became a buzzword in the 1970s. The cost of everything was going up. Gasoline edged toward a dollar a gallon, and a lot of people attributed it to the Vietnam War. Newspapers were not exempt, and the cost of newsprint rose as well as other factors in doing business. Newspapers that subscribed to both services were forced to make a choice of which one they wanted to keep. By this time, afternoon newspapers were beginning to make the change to becoming morning papers—being on the front porch to be read over breakfast instead of being there when the workers got home after a day in the office.

Then came Wednesday, June 2, 1982, another day in the office. I was working the night desk, a 3:00 p.m. to 11:00 p.m. shift. It seemed like minutes into my shift that I took a phone call from Seymour Raiz, managing editor of the *Columbus Citizen-Journal*, a Scripps-Howard newspaper a couple of blocks away from our office.

"You're going to have a story to match the photo out of Cincinnati, aren't you?" he wanted to know.

"What photo out of Cincinnati?" I asked.

Generally reporters knew when photographers were assigned to get pictures and transmit, even if it were in Cincinnati and I was running the state report in Columbus.

"The one where Scripps-Howard sold UPI," Seymour said.

"I'll check and get a story to you," I said in my usual manner, hanging up the phone. "John!" I yelled.

John came out of his office into the main newsroom area to join me at the telephoto desk, where I was checking the photo wire to see what Seymour had been talking about.

"What's up?" he asked.

I found the photo. I didn't like what I saw in the three-men-and-a-piece-of-paper-type photo.

"We've been sold," I stammered. "For a dollar!"

I don't think many people knew that behind the scenes, Scripps-Howard was looking for a buyer.

Chapter 43

John
June 1982
A Financial Downfall

"W hat's going to happen to us?" everyone wanted to know. Here I was, the state editor once again now that Ed DiPietro had been let go. As state editor, I was working with clients but still oversaw what was going on in the office. And now this.

"How should I know?" was my first reaction.

No one had notified me of what was going on at the corporate level. I was as much in the dark as anyone else was at that time. I put in a call to my boss John Payne, in Pittsburgh, our regional office, to see what he knew.

"You know as much as I do," he told me, but I often wondered how truthful he was.

Douglas Ruhe and William Geissler, co-owners of a cable TV company in the Nashville, Tennessee, suburb of Brentwood, had purchased United Press International, one of the nation's most prestigious news and information institutions. For one dollar! And assuming an enormous debt.

It would take us awhile to find out who Ruhe and Geissler were and how they worked.

"Just do what you normally do," I told my staff.

The staff, management, and clients had been though the scrutiny of Reuters when the British-based news agency was looking at the possibility of buying UPI when its financial plight first became known a few years earlier.

"How do you make scones?" was a question I often heard bantered around among my own staff. "What do they taste like?"

Those questions died as quickly as Reuters lost interest in UPI, more than likely because of the debt that Scripps-Howard had amassed.

In 1982, we continued to work as we had. One of the first things I did was check with Terry Bochatey, the photographer in our Cincinnati bureau who had transmitted the photo. He told me he had been summoned to the Scripps-Howard office to take photos and that no one had said anything about restrictions on transmitting. He sent the photo across the wires, thinking that a newsperson was writing the story and would send it to match the photo.

The transmission of that photo was the first we had heard of the sale—and to think we had to hear it from clients! I'm sure the same scene was repeated in UPI bureaus across the country.

Reporters in our headquarters office in New York began scrambling to get a story and calm clients while trying to learn their own fate.

Everyone was wondering what the next step would be. I was just as bewildered as the group I was assigned to lead.

"Everyone will stay on, and we will do the same quality of work we did before the sale," I assured them. I hoped I was right.

Not only did I have to reassure myself and my staff, I had to reassure our clients. It wasn't long until they were calling. "What's going on?" they wanted to know.

Here again I told them just what I had told my staff.

Our clients adopted a wait-and-see attitude. I was thankful that they were not rushing to dump the UPI service and sign up with the Associated Press, but then our sales representatives were in no hurry to sign new clients.

Occasionally a story about UPI would run on major wires, but it appeared to come from a news release from the new owners. Reporters wrote of other businesses experiencing difficulties. Would they soon be writing stories about their own employer and their own future?

Chapter 44

Sandi
Fall 1982
A Major Stumbling Block

When I married in the spring of 1974, two poodles came along with Red. We acquired a third one in early 1975. We lost one dog in 1977, and in late summer 1982, I lost the little one, Shane, the one who had adopted me the day I met him in 1973. The little fellow had grown to about five pounds and had attached himself to me. He had developed respiratory problems and had to be put down. I cried all the way home from the vet's office with the dog's body in the trunk of the car. I stopped at the bank where Red was working, and he told me he was getting me a female for my birthday, some six weeks off. Meanwhile, our remaining dog, Zeke, tried to comfort me.

Within days of losing Shane, I discovered a lump on the right side of my pelvis. I immediately called the doctor's office and made an appointment for the following Monday. But that morning the receptionist called to tell me the doctor was ill and not coming to work, and asked if I could reschedule. I started crying.

"What's wrong, Sandi?" she asked.

When I described the lump, she sent me to another doctor and rescheduled me for my family doctor. The appointment with that doctor and two with my regular family physician didn't produce any satisfactory results, so my family doctor sent me to a surgeon.

The surgeon discovered a fibroid tumor.

"Either it is or it isn't," he said of a possible malignancy. "We won't know until we operate."

He wanted me to be in the hospital on Monday morning.

"But we're going to Sandusky that day to see my husband's family," I began bargaining. "If you let me go, I promise I'll be there that evening."

He agreed.

I had had a couple of tests at the hospital before I was admitted, and had more after I was admitted. I had catheters inserted between my kidneys and bladder because the tumor was lying against the right kidney and it wasn't functioning at full capacity. I was scheduled for surgery Thursday.

Friday morning the surgeon stopped in to chat with me.

"I took out the tumor and had it biopsied," he said. "It was malignant and had metastasized to the ovaries. I had to go in and take out the ovaries and uterus."

He tapped the curved protector over my stomach.

"Ovarian carcinoma. I've been in touch with an oncologist, and we set up a chemotherapy regimen even before we closed you," he said.

I was devastated. Was I going to die? How long did I have? No, I wasn't going to let it get me down. I was going to fight for all I was worth. I was too young. I wasn't even forty. I had too much to live for. Besides, Red had just brought that female puppy home, the one he promised me for my birthday, which we celebrated a few weeks earlier.

Within a week I was released, and at the start of the next week, I began my chemo treatments at the hospital.

Thank goodness for my coworkers. They made the trek to our home on the far west side of the county to cheer me. They brought books. They brought pictures their kids drew in school.

John was creative. That summer I would stop at the juice bar in the lobby of the building and get a container of watermelon chunks.

"I tried to get you watermelon sherbet but couldn't find any," he said, handing me a cold container. "I hope you like rainbow sherbet."

"I'll eat it," I said, putting it in the freezing unit of the refrigerator.

It was one of the few items of food I could handle after a treatment. I could also get tomato soup down. Then I graduated to macaroni and cheese.

John was my savior during the next two years, and so were my coworkers. John scheduled me for days off when my monthly chemo treatment was planned. I'd work Sunday morning, go to the hospital that afternoon, have my IV treatment Monday, and go home Tuesday morning. Wednesday was a feature day, a day I could do as I wished. If I didn't feel like going to work, I didn't have to. I never missed a day of work other than the sick leave days after surgeries.

I had second-look surgeries in the fall of 1983 and again in 1984, when it was determined I was clean. I had been off work six weeks for the first two surgeries. I couldn't wait to get back to work after that third one. I had beaten cancer!

That led to my fellow workers giving me the nickname Sandlot—I had the determination of a sandlot ballplayer.

I still get called Sandlot today and use it as the basis of my e-mail address.

Chapter 45

John
Fall 1982
Keep On Keepin' On

My staff continued to work as though nothing had happened. They still covered the legislature and state government; wrote news stories, feature stories, and sports stories; compiled broadcast reports; and collected basketball and football scores.

With each day's report, they seemed to become more conscious of stories specifically for our clients. We occasionally noticed stories about UPI's financial problems in the report.

After the initial story of the sale, a few reporters in Tennessee turned their attention to who Douglas Ruhe and William Geissler were.

They found the two had little experience in the news field. They owned a Nashville, Tennessee, cable television company, but not many people knew anything about them.

The two also belonged to the Baha'i faith, which has its roots in Iran. Reporters who had grown up knowing journalism to be independent began questioning the basis of this religion and wondered if the new owners would try to infuse their beliefs into their new venture.

Their glib tongues soothed the questions.

Then came the revelations the two each had criminal records and arrests, followed by more questions and concerns and more glib talking.

They said the arrests stemmed from civil rights demonstrations and that Geissler had voluntarily served a federal prison term rather than register for the draft during the Vietnam War.

Our longtime leaders, who had struggled to keep the UPI name in front of readers, didn't trust the new leadership. Ruhe and Geissler wanted big names, well-known and well-respected journalists, to fill the top administrative spots.

The pair struck out. Longtime UPI folks left, and the big names turned them down. People they brought on were hired at salaries UPI leaders had never seen. Holding the line on expenses, or downhold in UPI language, didn't mean much to these guys. Even some of the new ones left not long afterward with golden-parachute packages.

I kept assuring our clients that things would eventually make a turn for the better and encouraged them to stay with us.

Behind the scenes, these new people were trying to form new business ventures, using new technology and trying to introduce it to the business of news. How much did they know about the news business? I knew through their limited experience they needed as much help as they could get. They had never gone head-to-head with a competitor to be the one to "get it first, but first get it right"—the UPI mantra.

While we tried to get news specifically for the clients, we started opening bureaus in outlying cities. That appeased some clients. Historically we had had offices in Columbus, Cleveland, and Cincinnati. Clients said they wanted a variety of datelines, more than the three Cs.

In late 1982, we opened a bureau in Youngstown and sent Rosemary Armao. Besides being a good writer, she was a self-starter.

After she had established a routine and had written some good stories, we opened a bureau on the other end of the state. Donna Davis left Columbus for northwest Ohio.

Both women were doing fantastic jobs, and the clients seemed pleased.

It was beneficial in other ways. Both Rosemary and Donna had gained valuable experience in Columbus and knew the routine. Since we had taken them out of Columbus (and didn't replace them), it was only natural that they handle some of the duties for the Columbus bureau.

We had fewer people in Columbus. Expanding technology meant we could forward phones to another bureau and have a shift covered by someone in a different city.

Later we opened a bureau in Dayton with a new hire, Mary Kane. The expansion in Ohio came to an end when we appeased another client who wanted more stories out of the Akron area in northeast Ohio; Jeanne Reall took her skills honed in Columbus to Akron.

It wasn't long before we had a hole in northeast Ohio. The UPI status was beginning to wear on Rosemary Armao. She and her family lived in Kent and she worked in Youngstown, a distance that could take up to an hour depending on traffic to commute to work. She moved with her extensive journalism knowledge and experience to the *Cleveland Plain Dealer*.

In the midst of all the expansion, Jay Gibian, who had taken the Ohio broadcast report to the status of being one of the best state reports in the company, wanted to work out of the Cleveland office, where he could be close to his aging mother in Akron.

All these expansions were costing money, and not much new revenue was forthcoming. Our report was widening, but on the national front UPI was sinking deeper into debt.

One thing I believed in—and practiced—was to put employees where they could do the best job. With this group of workers, I felt that I had excelled.

Chapter 46

Sandi
June 1983
Miss Ohio Pageant

John asked me in 1983 to go to Mansfield for the Miss Ohio Pageant, which was held the second week in June. For several years, we had had an arrangement with the *Mansfield News Journal* for one of their reporters to call us with results each evening. I thought it was a little unusual for him to send me out this time.

We had been under new owners for about a year when I was given the assignment. On the other hand, I had started chemo a few months before and had treatments every three to four weeks. Since I lost all my hair between my first two sessions, I was now wearing a wig.

I was honored to be asked to go out on a story. I knew I wasn't on the level of Lee Leonard, who had distinguished himself in the political field and was chosen to join the national press corps at the Republican and Democratic National Conventions.

When John told me I would be going, I called the woman at the *News Journal* and advised her I was coming, but I needed the names of people in charge so I could do some preview stories and be prepared when I arrived.

She gave me the name and phone number of the producer, who lived in Zanesville in eastern Ohio. I talked to him, and a couple of days later,

I received a thick packet. It contained photos and bios of each of the contestants and their phone numbers. I called the young women, and through these interviews I was able to put together a thumbnail sketch of each contestant and an accompanying preview story for weekend editions.

I went a day before the pageant began so I could attend a performance of the Ohio Light Opera Company, which was headquartered at the College of Wooster in the adjacent county. Ohio Light Opera selections were presented in a contemporary building, while the Miss Ohio Pageant was presented in a renovated movie palace-type theater that had opened in 1927.

By this time I had my own Radio Shack TRS-80 word processor, so I could write my story and file it from my motel room. To do this I had to dial a special toll-free phone number, and then put the phone receiver in rubber cups that were plugged into the word processor. My story would then be sent to the UPI office in Columbus.

The person working the desk at that hour, generally Jim Carter, would be on the lookout for my story so he could get it out to the newspapers and broadcast outlets.

I had to write fast to get a story on the evening's winners to our clients who were publishing morning papers and get a couple of paragraphs out for radio and TV stations for their 11:00 p.m. newscasts. Then I used the notes from the post-pageant news conference to write a story for the afternoon newspapers.

Not only did I write a story about the winners; I also wrote a review of the musical entertainment offered while the contestants were changing clothes for the different segments of the pageant.

When I wrapped up work for the day about two o'clock in the morning, I'd be getting hungry. The only place open close by was a twenty-four-hour greasy spoon across the street. I'd slip over and place a carryout order while keeping a watchful eye on what few customers were there. I usually ordered a sandwich, a piece of pie or cake, and a cup of coffee that I ate safely behind the locked door of my motel room.

I began planning on a trip to Mansfield every year. Our client newspapers were using everything I wrote about the pageant. I was enjoying myself.

One year the only room I could get in Mansfield was at the Holiday Inn adjacent to the theater because the motel where I usually stayed was being renovated and another one nearby was full. The Holiday Inn had an elevated walkway that connected the hotel to the theater.

I was unable to transmit from the phone in my room. The alternative was to take my TRS-80 and some change to the pay phone in the second-floor lounge of the theater. I transmitted from there with no problem. I was able to use the toll-free number so I didn't have to use my handful of quarters that I had just in case.

After I filed my story, I'd always call the office on its toll-free line just to make sure the story arrived in its entirety. Those nights I was the only one in that theater, and I thought I could hear my footsteps on the elegant carpet. I'd always look around just to make sure I *was* the only one there.

Chapter 47

John
1983
UPI Struggles

O ccasionally we'd see a story about UPI happenings on one of the national wires. That story would be of interest to the employees because we wanted to know our fate.

The goal of writing a story and sending it to clients is to get them to print the story in their paper to inform, educate, and enlighten their readers. I often wondered if readers understood the inner workings of what was going on with the company that provided the news they saw in their papers.

As I went through client papers we received every day in the mail, I began to see editorials and explanations of what would happen if UPI folded. Editors stressed the need for more than one source of news.

Having two news services kept both on their toes. Having only one would be a monopoly, some people claimed. A monopoly isn't good.

"You're the only game in town—what do you care? How do you feel about the job you do? Are speed and quality still as important?" were questions that were beginning to be raised.

Discussions took place in the Columbus office as well as interoffice chatter on the message wire.

Meanwhile, the debt increased. Something desperately had to be done. In spring of 1983, the first layoffs came. Those laid off were employees not protected by the Wire Service Guild. Reporters were safe at this time.

Owners Doug Ruhe and William Geissler wanted and needed investors, but the investments had to be on their terms and that didn't go down well with many people with money, so money wasn't coming.

The two were constantly seeking help, both in leadership roles and in financing. They called upon what they hoped was a financial genius: Luis Nogales from California. In his teen years, he had picked fruit with migrant workers in California; and in his adult life he had worked at Gene Autry's Golden West Broadcasting Corporation.

At one time he had talked about wanting to work with Ruhe and Geissler. Now he had his chance. He signed on as executive vice president. I don't know if he knew the full depth of what he was getting into.

Our owners wanted new equipment to be out in front in this fast-changing technological world, but it cost money. To make money, you have to spend money, and they were spending.

In an attempt to cut expenses, the pair had moved the corporate offices to Brentwood, a suburb of Nashville.

Employees were upset when they learned Ruhe and Geissler had negotiated an agreement to sell 11 million photos UPI owned to Bettman Archives for $1.1 million. Some of those photos dated back to the beginning of photography.

Other entities were sold, and payroll was covered this time around.

Negotiations continued in an attempt to get money. Foothill Capital Corporation in Los Angeles came through with a loan of up to $4 million, but loans have to be paid back with interest.

The debt only got worse, and Unipressers deep down began to worry.

Chapter 48

John
1984
Bankruptcy!

The financial picture didn't seem to be getting any better under Luis Nogales.

He obtained a large loan from Foothill Financial in Los Angeles so UPI could meet its obligations. The debt was growing at about $1 million a month.

It wasn't long until the news broke—UPI was filing for bankruptcy. Our paychecks identified UPI as DIP—debtor in protection.

It was Chapter 11 bankruptcy, one that would allow the company to reorganize. One positive move was putting the pension plans with the Pension Benefit Guarantee Corporation. That meant the pension plans were safe and the money would be there when the employees retired and applied for them.

More than a year after UPI went into bankruptcy, a Mexican communications executive, Mario Vasquez-Rana, bought UPI out of bankruptcy in a bidding war with Earl Brian, owner of Financial News Network.

Vasquez-Rana brought in Joe Russo, a Houston developer, for this new venture. I felt he brought in Russo to appease Americans who were skeptical of foreign ownership. Shortly after Vasquez-Rana became owner, the contract with the Wire Service Guild expired and he instituted work rules.

"What are work rules?" the staff started asking. Nobody really knew what work rules were, and we continued to work under an extension of the old contract.

Our clients were still skeptical of foreign ownership. They saw it as another American company being taken over by a foreigner, one who didn't even speak English. Some newspapers apparently didn't feel comfortable with foreign ownership, and they canceled their contracts with UPI and signed with AP. We were losing clients and losing money, and that would mean losing employees and producing less copy.

Chapter 49

Sandi
1985
Can Anything Else Go Wrong?

At times I think Murphy's Law followed me around: "If anything can go wrong, it will." I often thought that if I had a given amount of money every time Murphy's Law kicked in, I could have retired long ago.

This time I was hit with bad news from every side. In the spring of 1985, I was feeling great after finishing chemotherapy and my surgeries.

One day getting ready to leave for work, I decided to take a piece of misdelivered mail to the rightful owner. I had pulled into the driveway of that house to hand over the mail. One of the girls who lived there was leaving as I was getting into my car. She started backing up before I could get my car moving and backed into my car, taking out the grille.

At UPI we were in bankruptcy, and we never knew how long we would have a job or have a company.

Not only were we now reading of the financial problems at UPI, but we also were writing stories of the failure of Home State Savings and Loan of Cincinnati. I had transferred my funds from a bank to a savings and loan so I could gain a better interest rate. Where was my money? That's right! In Home State, which had recently bought out the little savings and loan I had chosen.

In Cincinnati, Home State invested $140 million in nonexistent securities, and customers were demanding their money. That reminded me of the runs on the banks prior to the Great Depression.

I was just short of panicking. I sat in the middle of the living room floor, crying.

"I'm recovering from cancer. My savings are in jeopardy. I don't know how long I'm going to have a job, and now my car needs to be repaired so I can go out and find a new job," I cried.

"I don't know how to help you," my husband said, letting me cry.

Home State went belly-up, but thanks to the state of Ohio, I didn't lose my money. The state dipped into its rainy-day fund and bailed out the financial institution.

But UPI was a different story. There was no bailout for UPI.

Chapter 50

John
1985
Money Woes Are for Real

The day my paycheck bounced was scary. We needed the money. We had bills to pay—house mortgage, car payment, insurance, utilities, food, and department store bills. Even though the four children were grown and on their own, we still slipped them money occasionally.

Not only did my paycheck bounce, but so did my expense check. Was the company going to make them good? Was this going to happen again next week? How long could we live on Patti's paycheck, which was a fraction of what I was bringing home? She was working full-time as a nurse at Westminster-Thurber Nursing Home.

That night we sat down and spread out the bills. Like many Americans, we were living from week to week. Who was going to get paid? House, car, and utilities had to be paid. We set aside an amount for food. The department store would get a minimum payment.

"How long is this going to go on?" Patti asked.

I shrugged. "I don't know."

I always seemed optimistic, but deep down I was beginning to get scared.

"I can always get a job at a newspaper," I said.

That was about the only thing I knew. I could write. With a little bit of training, I could handle the computers. I could handle just about any beat, but would I be happy starting all over again as a newspaper reporter? Would it be in Columbus, or would we have to move to another city?

I had another option. I could take an early retirement and get a UPI pension. Since I had served both as a reporter and in management, I was eligible for both the employee's pension and a management pension. That would help.

I was only in my fifties and too young to begin collecting Social Security. I definitely would need another job.

All these questions were weighing on my mind when we received a little reprieve the next day. Our income tax refund arrived. Patti and I breathed a little easier.

Most of my employees who were married had a working spouse and a second check coming in. They had bills too. The single workers were in a real bind. They didn't have that other paycheck to look to. They were panicky, like I was. Everyone was.

At UPI headquarters, executives scrambled to get money to issue us new paychecks. Another loan? Sell off another entity to meet the payroll? The story seemed to be repeating itself.

Chapter 51

John
1986
Not on My Shift

"Not on my shift" is a phrase I heard many times in my career. Employees were begging people not to die when they were working.

I kept trying to tell them to be like Boy Scouts and be prepared. To try to enforce what I was saying, in my spare time I would write obituaries and stash them in a drawer. In later years when we acquired computers, we were able to put them in a hold file, one that did not purge after forty-eight hours.

The person didn't always have to die for us to use the obituary. If that person were the subject of a major news story, we would have that obituary to use as background information.

One I wrote in the late 1960s and set aside was for Thomas "Yonnie" Licavoli of Toledo, a member of the Purple Gang. This was a Mafia-type gang whose turf spread from Toledo to Detroit and had ties to St. Louis. Licavoli had been sentenced to prison in 1933 for murder and had been in the Ohio Penitentiary ever since. He was paroled in 1972 when he was sixty-eight years old and spent his remaining days with family. Within minutes after we received the announcement from the Department of Rehabilitation and Corrections that Licavoli was to be released, we had a lengthy story moving with all the background. Staff members in other bureaus asked how we had so much so soon.

"We had an obituary written," I advised them.

The same thing happened when James Rhodes was seeking a court ruling as to whether he could run for another term as governor in 1974 after having sat out four years following his eight years in office. I had an obituary written and was waiting on Rhodes's decision. The day that Rhodes filed his request, I pulled the obituary out of the desk drawer and used that for a full-blown story within a matter of minutes.

Chapter 52

Sandi
1988
Jackie Presser

Regardless of how hard we hoped it wouldn't happen on our shift, inevitably it would.

With Mondays generally a slow news day, it seemed as though we welcomed a big story. One Monday about a year after I started at UPI, I was working on broadcast with Jay Gibian, who came aboard three months after I did, on the main desk. John by this time was taking Sunday and Monday off. Jay and I often worked the Monday day shift and routinely grumbled about how quiet it was and wished something would happen.

One Monday in the precomputer days was busier than usual. Around noon we learned of the death of one of our Congressmen in Washington. We scrambled to get information for the main story and sidebar, which consisted of comments from colleagues. I had plenty to write for broadcast that day.

Jay had the habit of working his eight hours straight through, while I took a break in the middle of my shift for a lunch hour. The contract said we had to work eight hours in a nine-hour period. I came in at 6:00 a.m., took a lunch hour, and left at 3:00 p.m. Jay came in at 7:00 a.m., worked eight hours straight, and also finished at 3:00 p.m.

That day we both left at 3:00 p.m., exhausted and feeling we'd earned our pay.

"Next time I start complaining on a Monday that I don't have fresh copy to work from, remind me of this day," I said, letting a deep breath slip out audibly as we trudged down the hallway together.

"I agree," Jay said.

Together, with the help of Lee Leonard in the Statehouse, we had pulled together a play-winning story. We all made phone calls to obtain information to add to what had been sent in or phoned in. That was on top of the regular work we did.

Fortunately the old beat-up Royal typewriters were easy to type on and we could work up speed—not like the Olivetti that showed up one day. I worked on it for one hour and went in search of the old Royal. The Olivetti keyboard was too steep and too stiff, and I couldn't work up a good rhythm. Whoever decided we needed new typewriters surely didn't work like we did.

I only wish we'd had obituaries written on prominent people in those days. We did later, and it helped.

In late July 1988, I was working the Saturday night shift. We were no longer a 24/7 bureau and were making use of technology by forwarding phones to another bureau and letting someone else do the work.

By this time in UPI history, we had several bureaus in Ohio, and those who staffed them took turns working different shifts. Since Columbus was no longer operating around-the-clock, we used the call-forwarding feature on the phones.

I had done a lot of work on this shift to help the person who would open up on Sunday. We were now closing the bureau at 1:00 a.m. Sunday and forwarding the phones to Chicago until whoever opened up on Sunday morning was able to take them back. Chicago would handle any middle-of-the-night phone calls, and the morning person could pick up the information. The main call on Saturday night/early Sunday morning was from the Ohio Lottery with expanded information from the evening drawing.

About five minutes before I was scheduled to leave, the phone rang.

On the other end was Pete Halpin, the press agent for Teamsters Union President Jackie Presser, whose office was in Cleveland, where he lived. I had spoken with Pete on many occasions when we were writing labor stories.

"Sandi," he said, "Jackie died awhile ago."

I knew Jackie Presser hadn't been well. Although deaths come at any time, they are still unexpected and come as sort of a shock.

As I took information from Pete, I was also sending an urgent message—Jackie Presser dead—to our national desk in New York and national broadcast desk in Chicago. I cleaned up my notes to forward to New York, which by this time had transmitted a one-paragraph bulletin and Chicago had run its broadcast item.

I forwarded my notes to New York along with Pete Halpin's phone numbers. When I was assured that New York had all it needed at this time, a little after 1:00 a.m., I finally forwarded the phones so I could go home. By that time in the Eastern time zone on Sunday, the only papers nearing deadlines are in the Mountain and Pacific time zones.

I turned out all the lights but one, locked the door, and headed to the elevator. Leaning against the wall as I descended from the eighteenth floor to the lobby of the Lincoln LeVeque Tower, I exhaled and said, "Jackie, you weren't supposed to die on my shift."

Chapter 53

John
1989
We Try Harder

In some aspects it looked like UPI might be going down, but in Ohio, we fought hard to stay afloat. UPI in Ohio was making money, but that wasn't the story in other areas.

We had an energetic young regional executive, Jamie Tailer, who came from a family of Chicago newspapermen. He brought back a couple of Ohio clients who had gone to AP and also signed a couple of papers who had been with AP forever.

It seemed as though he spent much time in northwest Ohio. Not only was he wooing newspapers, but he was also wooing Donna from the Toledo office. When Jamie left UPI, Donna soon followed him.

To fill the Toledo spot left open by Donna's leaving, I hired Jim Sielicki from the *Kenton Times* in northwest Ohio. I had been impressed with a headline he wrote for a story on the Falklands War: *The Empire Strikes Back*. He started working for UPI in March 1985.

Meanwhile, in New York, the office of president of UPI had become a revolving door. Some didn't even stay six months. They didn't bring a pocketful of miracles with them, but they left with a pocketful of money.

Then came a Saturday morning in the spring of 1988, and I got a phone call from the Columbus office.

"John, did you know we have a new owner?" asked the young woman working the morning desk. "Check the paper."

That day we learned through a short AP item in the *Dispatch,* now a morning paper, that Dr. Earl Brian had wrested control away from Vasquez-Rana to keep UPI viable. Paul Steinle became president.

Brian was a surgeon in the military during the Vietnam War and became involved in politics and business in California after his tour of duty. I figured a businessperson would be able to turn the company around where the newspeople couldn't.

In later years, we learned that Brian falsified company finances in order to get loans. He was tried and convicted and eventually sent to prison.

Steinle was news director of Financial News Network and brought along a management team with experience in turning companies around.

Under this new ownership, I was bumped up the ladder into sales, in hopes of stopping the loss of clients in neighboring states or perhaps slowing it somewhat.

Chapter 54

Sandi
1989
My Turn in the Legislature

Dan Crawford was a handsome young man not long out of college. He had worked for the *Youngstown Vindicator* in its Columbus office before he was hired at UPI to help Lee Leonard in the Statehouse. He would also be learning to work in the main bureau.

He was a good writer, but when it came to sending the stories to clients, he seemed a little skittish—like he was afraid to push the file button. In his brief stint with UPI, he worked well with others, but working by himself in the evenings was another story.

I had worked with him quite a bit, showing him how to send the stories to a particular wire and letting him do it. But being alone can often by a scary time. Several staffers have told of a major story that broke the first night they worked alone. With Dan, it was different story. He didn't have a breaking story. The first night he was by himself, he called me every time he wrote a story.

"What do I do next?" he'd ask.

"After writing the story and reading it to make sure you have no errors, you have to hit the define block button at the top and again at the bottom of the story, then hit the file button. That block of copy you have defined will be sent to the wire you designated in the top line, which we call the 'put' line," I told him.

I ate dinner, washed the dishes, and cleaned the kitchen, all with the phone to my ear. My husband just rolled his eyes and shook his head.

"Are you getting overtime?" he asked.

Dan only worked for us for a short time before he was laid off in one of the financial crunches under the new owners. He went back to legislative coverage for another news agency and was in the Statehouse when I was asked to join Lee Leonard in the current session. This was new work for me, but I knew I could do it. I was glad that John had the confidence in me that I could do something different. I had often wanted to work with Lee, but never let it be known. I figured John or whoever was in charge over the years would see what I could do and put me where I could do my best.

I think everyone in the bureau had been given the opportunity to work the legislature with Lee. It broadened our horizons and got us out of the dress-down routine. Instead of slacks and sweaters, I had to wear a dress. Men had to wear a tie. Most of the work was on Tuesday, Wednesday, and Thursday, with a 9:00 a.m. to 6:00 p.m. shift. Occasionally we had some late hours, especially when getting down to the wire to get a budget enacted and get legislation passed before the session ended.

Ohio's legislature was not a sixty- or ninety-day session, as in some states. At the beginning, bills were introduced and assigned to committees. Work didn't pick up until after the governor's State of the State address. Odd-numbered years meant a budget had to be enacted by June 30. Work was minimal during the summer and picked up again after Labor Day.

My first morning that January, I was assigned to cover a committee hearing. At that time, rooms had been created in every nook and cranny of the Statehouse to handle offices and hearing rooms. Every state representative and senator served on several committees. In these committee sessions, legislators heard from proponents, opponents, and interested parties as they worked on bills that would soon be taken to the floor for a vote.

The committee room where I was going was on the main level of the Statehouse. The press room was on one of the higher levels. I walked down the wide marble steps that perhaps Abraham Lincoln once trod. The front edge of the steps showed the wear of a century or more of use. They were bowed. I turned left to go down a half dozen more steps toward the hearing room. There I met Dan Crawford. We stood face-to-face. I told him I was on my way to my first assignment and that I was scared. My knees were weak. He put his hands on my shoulders and gave me a little kiss on the forehead.

"Good luck," he said.

Was that his way of paying me back for the help I gave him a year or so earlier?

That session I covered committee hearings that ranged from high school soccer to the death penalty to recycling. When Lee covered House sessions, I covered Senate. And vice versa.

I lost track of Dan after awhile, and I was in shock the day in early June 2008 I read his obituary. The accompanying picture was one of him in the era I came to know him, but the obituary did not list a cause of death.

Chapter 55

John
1989
From Writing the News to Selling It

C hanges on the news side began catching up with me. We had gone through a string of regional execs, a nice word for salesmen. We'd had several in that capacity in the Columbus office who were responsible for sales throughout Ohio. None of them lasted long. In these waning days, I was asked to be a salesperson.

"John, you know this state and the newspapers probably better than anyone," I was told when I was offered the position. After all, I had been in Ohio more than twenty years and with UPI for thirty.

It was a long way from a reporter just out of college chasing after a little-known Massachusetts senator who wanted to be president to selling newspapers on the benefits of having the UPI wire in its office even as UPI was going downhill.

What were the benefits? Ohio had a stable of solid reporters, a staff who had worked together for twenty years or more. They were good writers and had a wealth of knowledge at their fingertips. They could pick up a phone, punch in a number, and do an interview. At times, they didn't even have to look up a phone number. I think Sandi could make all the calls on a basketball or football score-gathering night and never look up a number, yet she obtained scores from nearly every school in the state.

UPI was also beginning to work at unbundling the package. Until now, a newspaper or radio or TV station had to buy the full package. More copy hit the wastebasket than was used in the paper or on the air. It was a waste of paper, and newsprint was one of the biggest expenses. By unbundling, newspapers, radio, and TV could get only what they wanted. Each story carried an eight-digit code that identified it according to category. If a newspaper wanted just roundups of the American or National League in baseball instead of individual game stories, that's what they'd get.

It seemed so simple, and the reporters and writers soon knew the coding backward and forward.

Early in this position, I was able to get some clients to renew their contracts.

The first newspaper I visited to talk about renewing was the *Bucyrus Telegraph-Forum*, the paper that gave Sandi her start in journalism. I met with the publisher, Jim Croneis, and the news editor, Don Wynn. We sat in Croneis's office around a well-worn oak table. The AP had been trying to woo this newspaper, sending out literature as well as a representative to their office.

In the end, they renewed with UPI, saying that "Sandi Latimer and John Kady are like old shoes, and we're comfortable with you."

Then it was on to Bryan in northwest Ohio. That's where one step north puts you in Michigan and one step west in Indiana. I had a meeting with Linda Freed, editor of the *Times*. This again wasn't a hard sell. She didn't like AP and said she would stick with UPI.

I started with responsibilities in Ohio and soon was given parts of Pennsylvania, Indiana, West Virginia, and Kentucky. Not long after that, I was named vice president of sales for the entire Midwest.

I kept my office in Columbus while I traveled. I was in my midfifties when I took on this new task. Somehow it seemed something to keep me young.

Chapter 56

Sandi
1989
Ethics

I never knew what I would encounter when I walked into the office. Coming back to work after vacation in 1989 is one example. I was not quite in the mood for work, and people were asking what we did, where we went, did I have pictures. We had a motor home, and Red and I traveled with our white toy poodles, which by this time had grown to a brood of seven.

I dreaded the first day back—going through all that mail and messages that had accumulated during the past two weeks. This time I found a box addressed to me underneath the mailboxes. I hadn't ordered anything. This box was from a local gift shop.

I opened it and found a short note of thanks from a doctor I had recently interviewed for a story.

"I can't accept this," I said to John.

"Why not?" he asked.

"You know reporters shouldn't accept gifts from people they interview," I said. "It's not ethical."

I hadn't taken ethics in college, but I had learned enough over the years to know what is right and what is wrong.

I had decided I wanted to do a story about how a patient talks with his doctor. I had plenty of experience in that area when I went through my ordeal in 1982, but I needed a doctor to interview.

In 1982, I had been diagnosed with ovarian cancer and undergone two years of chemotherapy.

My oncologist and I got along well, and I kept a journal—my first one ever and at the age of forty. In it I wrote of my feelings, actions, reactions to my drugs, and any questions I raised between doctor's appointments and treatments.

I didn't want to rely on that. I needed a doctor. I had been doing some volunteer work for the cancer hotline, 1-800-4CANCER, taking and fulfilling requests. It was located at the Ohio State University Hospitals, but closed around the time the James Cancer Hospital was built. I then volunteered at the main hospital. I asked the volunteer director if she knew of anyone I could interview for the story. I kept asking people.

Eventually I made contact with Dr. Nelson Kraus, a medical reporter on a local TV station. It was better than nothing. I figured since he interpreted medical topics for the viewer, he could talk to my level.

I met with him one evening and had a wonderful interview. It was easy to write the story. I had made arrangements through our New York features desk to do the story, so it would be sent there to move nationally.

The box contained a variety of snack crackers and candies and contained a note from Dr. Kraus thanking me for the opportunity to appear on the Oprah Winfrey TV program.

What happens after the story is transmitted to clients is up to the recipient. Do they use it or do they pass? After a newspaper, radio, or TV uses the story, it's hard telling what the public does with it.

In the case of this story, someone from Oprah Winfrey's staff had seen the story—did a Chicago newspaper carry it?—and got in touch with the doctor and invited him to be on her show. Wow! I'd never had that happen before.

I felt better about accepting his gift since it wasn't a thank-you for writing the story. I still shared the goodies with my coworkers.

Book 3

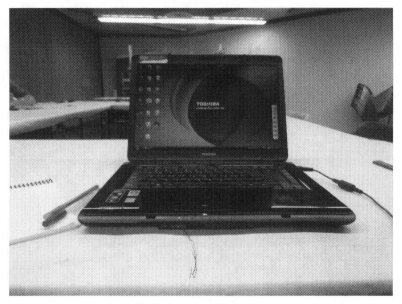

Photo by Sandi Latimer

1990–Today

Chapter 57

Sandi
1990
After UPI

U PI began a fast downward spiral in the summer of 1990.
I had planned a three-week vacation in late July and early August
and was assured that talk of getting a new computer system would not
affect Columbus until much later. UPI was the farthest thing from my
mind the three weeks we spent in Wisconsin with the dogs. We arrived
home twelve hours before we had planned. I had a phone message that
I was to report to work Sunday afternoon rather than Monday morning.

"We now have to log on to get onto the computer," the Toledo staffer
Jim Sielicki said in his message. "I'll stick around long enough to walk
you through it."

That was kind of him. I had done the same for several people over
the years.

When I arrived in the office and got settled with Jim's help from
Toledo, I learned that all the summer interns had been let go. The
tension was thick. No one knew what was going to happen.

"Do you have your résumé updated?" was a common question.

"I don't have a résumé," was the response. "I always thought I would
retire from here."

Many of us were in that group. I had a résumé that I had written years earlier. I had worked with the Association of Women in Communications on its annual JobHunt program for several years. AWC began as Theta Sigma Phi, a journalism honorary society, the feminine counterpart of Sigma Delta Chi in the days of segregated membership in organizations. That all changed in the mid-1960s, after the Civil Rights Act was passed. Once-segregated organizations opened membership to the opposite sex. Theta Sig decided to change its name to get away from the Greek letters and let people know what the organization was about. Sigma Delta Chi (SDX) was changing its name about the same time—to the Society for Professional Journalists—and opened its membership to women.

I had been asked to join Theta Sig after just two quarters of journalism classes and working on the student newspaper at Kent State. I was honored to be considered, especially since the invitation came from one of my professors. "Lady Bird Johnson is a Theta Sig," I told my mother, who had not wanted me to go Greek. "It's not a sorority; it's an honorary."

The first name change was Women in Communication, Inc., or WICI, and when the headquarters moved from Texas to near Washington, it became AWC. Its membership stayed gender-specific, although men were welcome. The group in Columbus held an annual JobHunt, a daylong program with workshops on how to find jobs, how to write résumés, and how to handle interviews.

What I learned there I passed on to my colleagues, who were wondering what their future held.

Not long after Labor Day, I was working an unusual 9:00 a.m. to 6:00 p.m. shift, picking up a variety of work on different desks. David Harding arrived around four o'clock to work the night desk. I was getting some broadcast work done ahead for him before I left. He would be handling the tasks of both the main desk and broadcast desk for a couple of hours. By this time, we were trying to do the same amount of work, but with fewer employees. Staffers in other bureaus were often asked to pitch in.

The phone rang.

I said, "UPI Columbus. Sandi Latimer speaking," my standard greeting.

The caller was our state editor, Tom Burnett, who now worked in Cleveland. How things had changed over the past twenty-two years. Much of it could be attributed to the computer. The state editor had always worked in the main office. Now Tom was working in Cleveland. He and his wife both had family in northeast Ohio, and with a toddler, the child would be close to grandparents.

Tom wanted to talk with David.

I didn't intentionally listen to the conversation, but I could tell from David's tone of voice that it wasn't good. He hung up and turned to me.

"It's been nice working with you the last seventeen and a half years," he said, so soberly I thought he was about to cry. "I just got laid off."

I ran around the bank of printers to where David sat and put my arms around his neck and hugged him. The family was breaking up—the family I had come to embrace since 1968. For me, it started that Thanksgiving when I volunteered to work a holiday to let others be with family. I was so surprised when the teletype operator came to work a little after noon carrying plates covered with aluminum foil— my Thanksgiving dinner his wife prepared for me. Now that's family!

Résumé writing began to take up much of our time. After David's last day, he would come to the office to work on his résumé and job hunt.

"You do it that way?" sports editor Gene Caddes asked as I helped him with a résumé.

"Write out United Press International; don't use UPI," I advised. "People don't know what UPI is. Do you know how many phone calls we get for UPS?"

John walked in one day with a box of résumés he had printed downstairs at InkWell. He handed me one to read.

I looked over it and then looked at him. "John, where do you live?" I asked. He gave me the address. "Where did you and Joyce live when you split up?" He told me.

"Toss these out," I said. "You have the wrong address. You used the address where you and Joyce lived, not where you and Patti live. Don't you know you're supposed to proofread these things before you have them printed? It's like proofreading and editing a story before you send it out."

I had been trying to work with people in other Ohio bureaus about editing. No one appreciated editing as I did.

"What do you do when you come across a misspelled word or something that doesn't sound right?" I'd ask.

I suppose if I'd spoken with them face-to-face instead of over the phone, I'd have gotten a blank stare.

"Didn't you take editing in college?" I asked, thinking back on my two courses of editing in college, both of which were so helpful all these years later.

"I didn't take editing because I didn't want to be an editor," was one reply.

I thought back to the time I was proofreading stories before sending them out.

"You should be a book editor," Jay told me as he watched how thoroughly I was working. What a compliment from someone who didn't always agree with me.

I also wondered why John had ordered so many résumés. He must have had five hundred in that box.

"I'm going to give them to a headhunter," he said.

"They don't know you and the type of work you can do," I argued.

"I didn't know you and didn't know what you could do, and we worked out all right, didn't we?" he asked.

"That's not the issue," I maintained.

Many jobs are not advertised; one finds them through networking with people in the field. I had a wide network thanks to membership in AWC and also Business and Professional Women, which I had joined in 1965, as well as some of the people I had met over the years in public relations positions. I had also joined Ohio Newspaper Women's Association and Ohio Professional Writers. I was the only person in the office who held a professional membership. I knew many people in a plethora of positions.

"Does it matter?" people have asked. Such memberships provided me with an edge. I could tap into job banks the organizations maintained, something people without such membership could not. I had a network I could use. If or when I had a question about something, I could ask someone in another organization.

A couple of weeks later, I was working night broadcast and got a call from Jay in the Cleveland office. I had worked with him for twenty-two years, most of them in Columbus, and never had much of a conversation with him. We didn't have much in common, but this night he wanted to talk.

"I wish I were more like you," he said. "You saved your money and lived frugally." Well, not quite frugally, but I was resourceful with my funds both before and after marriage. It was the way I was brought up. My father had always said, "If you can't pay cash for it, you don't need it." I married a man who was much the same.

"Me," he continued, "I had to have all the bells and whistles."

He was the first one in the office to have a computer and was using e-mail when others hardly knew what it was.

A short time before he called me, he had been notified he was being laid off. We talked for an hour and a half. I got little done that night. I even wondered if clients, what few we still had, would notice. Normally Jay commented, often not in complimentary ways, on our work, both quality and quantity. Would he care tonight?

Now I was getting scared. I had only three months seniority on Jay. I knew the next round of layoffs would get me. I had to act and act fast.

The company was on its last legs as we knew it. Now in its eighty-third year, we were beginning to wonder how much longer it could last.

We had staff all over Ohio. At the client level, clients were now able to get just what they needed and wanted. That saved many trees. Over the past few years, we had lost so many clients and cut the income. We laid off employees and that cut the output.

By this time we were faced with a dilemma. A proposal was put forth: take a 35 percent pay cut or lose the company. If the Wire Service Guild, of which I was no longer a member, rejected the offer, the company would go out of business. If it were approved, we would continue to operate. It was a Guild vote. I was working for the company, but I had no vote. Those allowed a vote were workers in good standing as of a certain date, and that was before the layoffs began. My future was in the hands of many people, some no longer working for the company.

I was still volunteering at the Ohio State University Hospitals one day a week. I now worked in the Prep Center, preparing file folders for the nurses to use with patients who were getting ready for surgery.

While going from the parking garage to the volunteers' office to report in, I ran into a longtime friend, David Irwin, who was now working in the hospital's media office.

"How's it going?" he asked.

I felt as though I knew him well enough and long enough that I could spill my guts. I told him everything that had happened in recent weeks and put enough emotion into it that I was almost in tears. I had grown to love UPI, and love my work, my opportunities, my fellow workers in Columbus, in Ohio, throughout the country. Now that family, that security, that life was breaking up. and I couldn't control it.

"We have an opening in our office," David said.

I worked my four-hour volunteer shift and then went to work at UPI that evening. When I got home. I hauled out my typewriter—I now had an electric one—and started to type my résumé. I worked until I was too tired to hold my eyes open. Red was working a third shift, and my dogs were smart enough to know that when the sun goes down and the lights come on, it is time to go to bed.

When I finished, I had a résumé typed and in a manila envelope addressed to David at his office at the hospitals. I had a cover letter attached to the résumé and a brief note to David to send this wherever it had to go.

The next night after work, I started going through dresser drawers, filing cabinet drawers, desk drawers, and the hall closet, looking for the tear sheets I had brought home over the years. I needed them now to put into a portfolio. I included the two stories I did on my battle with cancer—the one I wrote when I returned to work six weeks after my surgery (the one everyone called therapy to get me back to work) and the one I wrote when I passed my five-year survival period.

Other items included a copy of the story on parents of pregnant teens and the complimentary letter I received. In that portfolio were a variety of stories—features, news, legislative, whatever I could quickly scrounge up. I found a notebook in the basement and went out in the middle of the night to buy page protectors at a twenty-four-hour discount department/grocery store a couple of miles away.

I shared the information with my coworker David (I still had trouble calling him a former coworker). He also sent in a résumé. We both received calls for interviews. I got a callback for a second interview.

"I can do that," I said when the people talked with me about writing news releases and interacting with media people, putting them in contact with patients and physicians who could discuss procedures. "The three Ps," David Irwin said when I interviewed with him.

I was taking a writing test when someone slipped into the cubicle and put a hand on my shoulder. I looked around and saw Jane Gordon, a young woman I had met several years ago when she was doing a public relations internship at Bob Evans Restaurant's corporate office. I hadn't seen her in years.

"Jane, it's nice to see you again," I said in a solid greeting as we hugged. Then somewhat sheepishly I asked, "Do you work here?"

"Just across the aisle," she said, turning and pointing to the cubicle behind me. We chatted for a while, then she said, "I have to get back to work, and you have to finish your writing test. Good luck."

Again we hugged. I left that day with hope. I felt I had done well on the interviews and knew I had done well on the writing test.

I had some practice in writing news releases. I had seen all kinds of releases coming across the UPI desk in twenty-two years. I saved some good ones, including some I considered not so good but that had gotten my attention, and some I set aside and read when I had time and could look for the lead. I used those examples when I put together publicity clinics for organizations when they asked about how to get their event publicized. Since I had worked in several phases of communications—newspaper, radio, wire service—I felt I knew plenty to tell people how they all worked. I developed confidence.

I waited. I worked and waited. Guild members were voting. I saw messages from people around the country on their views of the vote and the current conditions. Not all were uplifting. People were mad, hurt, scared. The vote was tabulated. The question passed. UPI workers would take a 35 percent pay cut.

Part of me was thankful. I could survive on that lower rate, but could others? Why couldn't they just have voted not to take it and pull the plug? I was on one side of the fence, then the other. "Pull the plug, let it die, and let me get on with my life." "Approve the pay cut and let me work."

I was working a day shift when the vote was announced. I got a call that evening from David Irwin offering me the job at OSU. I accepted. I called UPI, and the call was answered in Cleveland, where the night operation was being handled. We had to be creative with work shifts now that we had so few people. I told Rich Exner that I was just offered a job at OSU Hospitals in medical communications and I accepted. I would start December first. I would leave UPI November 30.

"How many résumés did you have out?" Rich asked. I could almost hear his chin hit the floor when I replied, "One."

"It was the first time since I was a junior in college that I went looking for a job," I said. After I begged for an internship in the spring of 1964, I had been given jobs. I never had to go looking again. Twenty-six years. Times had changed in the job search process.

I couldn't cut my ties to UPI completely. December 1 was in the middle of the high school sports season. Football championships had just been decided, and the high school basketball season had begun around Thanksgiving weekend. If I left entirely, who would do the sports scores?

I started at UPI in the middle of March of 1968, the weekend of the state basketball tournament. I worked the first Friday night of the 1968 football season. I knew from my past jobs in radio that the wire services ran a list of scores. But I didn't know how they got them until that night. I helped, but I think I watched more. I learned. The next Friday night, Mason Blosser, with whom I was working, rolled his chair away from the desk and said, "It's all yours."

It was all mine for the next twenty-five years. I learned where all the high schools were or who I could call to get the scores. I had a reputation for a long list. Once we measured the list of scores, and the paper stretched from one side of the room to another.

One of my contacts compared my list of scores to that of AP. "You're far ahead of them," he would tell me.

Gene Caddes, the sports editor, once complained he couldn't find a particular school on my list.

"It consolidated with another school this year," I told him, pointing out the new name. "I missed that school, too, when I was getting scores from that area and had to ask about it."

My love of high school sports wouldn't let me leave this job. I felt attached to those scores. I worked out an agreement with John to come back on football and basketball nights to do scores.

It was unusual slipping into the office around nine thirty at night. Only the security guard was visible in the building. The UPI office was in a different location now. The suite on the eighteenth floor wasn't necessary. Only a couple of people were still working in Columbus. I'd look around and read stories of UPI progress.

But it wasn't the same anymore. I did the same type of work and still maintained my phone friendship with people I called for scores. How much did they know about what I was doing or what UPI was doing?

I did score gathering until the start of the football season of 1993. We were going to go to Myrtle Beach in late September. I didn't want to start the season and miss a week. It wouldn't be fair to what few clients UPI still had. In twenty-five years, no one else had learned to do this task. I finally cut my ties to UPI—or did I? My key ring still has keys to the UPI office and the front door of the building where UPI had its office.

Chapter 58

John
1990
A Switch in My Career

My duties kept expanding. First Ohio, then the surrounding states, and eventually I was named a vice president of sales and roamed the country.

On one trip to Chicago I stopped at the UPI bureau, and the news editor and I rented a car and drove to Satellite Broadcasting. The person we met with had worked at WBNS Radio in Columbus years ago. At that time the studio was a couple of floors above the UPI office. It was time for a little reminiscing.

I was amazed at the operations. The company was made up of several radio station studios, each one producing a different genre of music. I noticed a UPI printer in each little station. The personality in that station would strip the wire—tear off the copy—and sort it. This information would be inserted between cuts of music. Lots of small radio stations subscribe to that service since it cuts down on the number of employees it has to hire. I got that contract renewed.

How well I remember my first trip to New York. I flew into LaGuardia and took a taxi to the UPI bureau in Manhattan. The salesperson, Joan Meisenhelder, and I took a cab to the offices of what was going to be a new daily sporting newspaper, the *National*. The office was on the third floor of the building, which also housed the famed supper club 21. We were meeting with Frank Deford, a onetime contributing writer to *Sports Illustrated* and author of the book *Everybody's All-American*. I had read the book and seen the movie starring Dennis Quaid, Jessica Lange, Timothy Hutton, and John Goodman. It was about a fictional Heisman trophy winner whose professional career became sidetracked by outside influences.

I had written sports myself over the years. I covered basketball star Jerry West when we were students at West Virginia University. I wrote numerous Baltimore Colts stories and some features about the Baltimore Orioles. In Columbus I shared game-day duties for the Ohio State football coverage. I knew Deford and I would hit it off.

"Was the book based on the life of Charlie 'Choo Choo' Justice?" I asked. Justice was a running back for the University of North Carolina in the fifties.

"No," he replied, "but I got a call from a guy who won a Heisman at Louisiana State University."

"Oh, that had to be Billy Cannon," I said, surprising him with my knowledge.

His book was based on a fictional player at UNC, but in the movie, the location was changed to LSU.

It didn't take us long to map out an outline for a contract that even included a horse race wire along with the regular sports wire, news briefs, news photos, and breaking news stories. The contract was worth $5 million for five years. My commission was $92,000, and Joan's was $65,000.

Joan and I celebrated with champagne at 21.

Never heard of the paper? It went belly-up the following year.

I also had a good experience in Boston with the *Christian Science Monitor*, which was trying to cut costs. The paper had brought in several consultants and had been using AP but wasn't publishing much wire copy. Most of it ended up in the trash can.

"We can design a wire for you, giving you only what you want and need, and it will save you hundreds of dollars in paper costs alone," I said as I explained how the coding system we used could work for them.

The two sides agreed on a thirty-day test period.

I met with then UPI owner Earl Brian in Washington, which was now the UPI headquarters. We made several trips to Boston to see how it was going. On one trip we even found a bar named Cheers, and by the time the thirty days was up, everyone knew our names.

By the end of that test period, UPI had the contract for service, and the *Christian Science Monitor* had already thrown AP out. The revenue for this service was not nearly as much as it was for the *National*, but it came at a time when UPI was struggling financially. The public relations value of this contract: priceless!

I didn't do so well on a trip to San Francisco. Both the *Chronicle* and the *Examiner* told me they were in no position to add any services, but I wasn't deterred.

Just outside the door I picked up a gay-oriented newspaper. I found the number for the newspaper and called for an appointment. When I arrived, I went over a plan showing how UPI could send them gay-oriented news from all over the world through the custom coding process. The paper signed up on the spot.

As my responsibilities grew, so did other opportunities. We had often vacationed in North Carolina, where I had once been offered a job at a weekly newspaper. I couldn't see myself stepping down to a reporter's position. I turned down an offer from AP in Columbus. It just didn't seem right.

Vacations became a little more exotic. One summer Patti and I jetted off to Ireland. It was a far cry from North Carolina, or even family reunions back in the West Virginia hills.

At the company level, things still weren't going so well. With UPI on the edge of a second bankruptcy filing, I was offered a buyout. That was in 1993.

I accepted the offer and left UPI after thirty-four years.

"I was employed by UPI for thirty-four years and never worked a day in my life," I said many times. I enjoyed what I did, and it never did seem like work.

I was now engaged in a job search myself. I took a job in telemarketing for Sears. I would make telephone calls trying to set up appointments for salespeople to visit the home to estimate costs for replacing home siding, windows, or kitchen cabinets.

It was a far cry from writing about plane crashes or selling the wire service. Surprisingly I was happy with that job. I was selling. I was working regular hours, going home every evening and leaving the job behind me. I was also getting paid regularly and didn't have to worry about my checks bouncing.

But UPI was never far from my mind. I had a computer at home and e-mail. I joined the Downhold group and received regular messages from former UPI people. I also had an occasional e-mail or phone call from my former employees. We just couldn't sever those ties.

I worked at Sears for ten years. I was nearing seventy years of age. Health issues crept up. Diabetes had always been a problem. Then heart conditions arose. I had a skin cancer removed. And a stroke and a heart attack at the same time.

When I left Sears, I decided to return to writing. My first idea was to write a book. Surely I had a wealth of stories from which I could draw.

My first endeavor was a fictional story drawn on my two years in the air force on Okinawa. I wrote *A Sentry's Saga on Okinawa* and shipped it off to Publish America.

My next move was to get into the freelancing arena, and I chose to follow the video slot machines at race tracks and would offer stories to *Blood Horse* magazine in Lexington, Kentucky.

When my book was published, I got a call from Sandi. She invited me to go with her to a writing group. I kept writing. I pulled stories together from my early years at UPI—following Kennedy, covering the civil rights movement on the Eastern Shore, and Muhammad Ali in his fight with the draft board.

In 2009 I again turned to Publish America for the book *From Kennedy to Kent State: A Reporter's Notebook*.

I'm still writing, drawing on my experiences from stories I covered and from events that happened and left an impression on my mind.

Although I am aging, I don't want to admit it—but the vision isn't as good as it used to be and the phone has larger numbers. I don't use a computer much anymore, but my daughters do help me with that when I need it.

I'm fortunate I can still pick up the phone and call my old UPI friends.

Chapter 59

Sandi
1990 and Beyond
My New Paths

I worked at Ohio State for eight years. In 1998, we began to see some financial changes. I noticed it in our office, where my coworkers covered various departments much as a news reporter has a beat. I had started in media relations and worked with several departments, following their work and seeing what I could offer to the news media. I also worked with the marketing section, which also had people servicing the departments by making brochures about procedures.

We media people shared information with the marketing representatives, who worked the same departments we did. I could see some changes coming. By this time I was doing a variety of writing: writing and publishing the staff newsletter *Newsline* every week, compiling several sections of the *College of Medicine Journal*, and writing and overseeing the recording of the on-hold phone messages. Some of the people were working part-time, especially the women with young children.

As editor of the staff newsletter, I had information several days ahead of everyone else. Our department director's office was within coffee-smelling distance of the chief executive's office. I had seen layoffs in several departments and watched as many of our people went part-time.

I was thinking about asking if I could go part-time, but I didn't have details planned out.

Departments were cutting down the amount of work they were asking our office to do. Less work coming into our department created much free time. If I asked to go part-time, what days would I work and what would I find to do with the other days?

The last Monday in October, I was summoned to meet with my department director in Human Resources.

"We're abolishing your job as of today," I was told. "You will get one month's pay."

I had seen it coming but didn't want to believe it. I took it calmly. I didn't kick, scream, or fight. By the time I returned to my office, I was out of the computer as though I had never been there.

I cleaned out my office the next day and went into job-search mode. My computer at home was out-of-date. I didn't even have e-mail, that's how antiquated my computer was. I used my nephew's computer, the computer at the library, or whatever I could.

Despite a few tears and the feeling "this can't be happening to me, but it is," I slowly got on with my life.

I tapped into my network. I called former coworker Lee Leonard, with whom I had worked for more than twenty years. He left UPI a month after I did for the *Columbus Dispatch*, where he was still in the legislature. Did he know of any openings?

Within a month I had a job with Hannah News Service. It published a newsletter five days a week with legislative and state government news. It was part-time in the sense that I worked a few hours Monday and Friday, and full days Tuesday, Wednesday, and Thursday when the legislature was in session with committee hearings and floor sessions.

I also answered an ad for a part-time sports clerk for the *Columbus Dispatch*. The duties were compiling high school sports scores. I wanted that job to get back into the high school loop I had missed since 1993.

A couple of months after taking the job at Hannah, I was offered the part-time position at the *Dispatch*. It didn't interfere with the hours I was working at Hannah, and the work at the two offices didn't conflict.

If I didn't write at the *Dispatch*, I could write for anyone else. I accepted those terms.

I was back downtown again. I could ride the bus and not worry about parking. And I could take a walk on my lunch hour. A couple of times I ran into Gene Caddes, doing the same thing I was doing. He had left UPI for a position in the Legal Department of the Bureau of Workers Compensation. One day when we met on a street corner, he was grumbling about some writing.

Apparently he had produced something and got some praise about his writing.

"With those kinds of skills, you should be in the public information office," someone had told him.

"I put on my résumé that I worked for UPI," he contended, then told me the person he was talking with said she didn't know what UPI meant.

The work at Hannah wasn't really the type of writing I desired. It was more "he said this, she said this" in committees. I didn't have the flexibility I desired. After two years I was sending out résumés again.

"I remember you," I heard the editor of the *Columbus Messenger* Westside edition say when she called in response to my résumé that landed on her desk. She explained that she went to Ohio State and was a reporter for the *Lantern*, the student newspaper. She had the hospital beat one quarter and worked with me on a couple of stories. She even showed me my old business card in her Rolodex. She offered me the Columbus schools beat for the independent free weekly newspaper that had five editions, one of which was in my neighborhood. I accepted.

I had had an offer from another weekly newspaper covering another school district, but I would have to quit the *Dispatch*. I couldn't quit the *Dispatch*, where I was working nineteen hours a week, for a job that would be one story a week. The economics didn't compute, and I wasn't one who could handle two or three hours' work a week.

I enjoyed both the *Dispatch* and the work at the *Messenger*. I was making new friends and doing different things. I had been sent to the Columbus Cultural Arts Center on a story for one of the other editors at the *Messenger*. I discovered that the writing group, the Ohio Writers

Guild, was meeting in that same room on a different day. I went to check it out and kept going back. Some people in this group were writing fiction, something I had wanted to learn. I hoped they could help me, inspire me.

In the summer of 2002, Carol Wooten, whom I had met at the McDowell Senior Center on a story assignment, asked me to join her walkers in a trip through Green Lawn Cemetery. I wanted to go because the volkswalking friends I'd been associated with for about ten years wanted a walk in the cemetery.

"George, Sandi's a writer," Carol kept telling our tour guide.

I motioned to Carol to hush up.

"George, Sandi's a writer," she said again.

"George, why is she doing this?" I asked the tour guide.

"We need someone to edit our newsletter," he said.

After our tour, I stopped in the office and asked about the editorship. I could do it as a volunteer, putting it out three times a year. I had returned to volunteering after I left Hannah and went to work for the *Columbus Messenger*. I followed through on a story in the *Dispatch* where FirstLink, a twenty-four-hour information and referral system, needed volunteers to help answer phones and assign people to food pantries. I was assigned a schedule that first day.

By early the next year, that volunteer position at the cemetery turned into an offer to become the volunteer coordinator on a part-time basis, ten hours a week.

"Who are my volunteers and what do they do?" I asked the general manager, Linda Burkey.

"You have to recruit people to become volunteers and create jobs for them," she said.

I was now working three part-time jobs—the *Columbus Messenger*, the *Columbus Dispatch*, and Green Lawn Cemetery, the second-largest cemetery in Ohio.

I was also doing things at strange hours—like grocery shopping. One evening in early 2004 as I rounded a corner of the aisles at Meijer, I ran into Patti Kady. Gee, I hadn't seen her in a few years. We had exchanged Christmas cards, but I hadn't seen her or John and hadn't heard from either of them for so long. I almost didn't recognize her. Her hair was beginning to turn gray. I suppose mine was about the same.

"John had a heart attack and a stroke at the same time," she told me. I was shocked.

"How is he?" I stammered.

"He's in Franklin Woods, the rehabilitation center on Clime Road," she said.

The next day I drove the few miles to Franklin Woods and wound my way down the hallways to John's room.

"Hi, babe," he said when I walked in the room, where an aide was working to get shoes on him and get him on his feet.

"I hired her a long time ago," he told his aide.

"Karen Brokaw said hi," he said to me.

I was surprised. I didn't know he knew Karen. I hadn't thought of her in years. I had met her in 1977 when I went to exercise classes at the Hilltop YMCA; I learned aerobic dancing from her and started running.

"I haven't seen her in forever," I said. "How did you know I knew her? What is she doing now?"

"Her mother is down the hall," John said.

I knew then that John had been talking and somewhere my name came up.

I couldn't let John see how shocked I was that he was not the same person I had last seen in 1990. He had a mobility problem and needed help getting around. I hoped he would overcome this. *His mind is good*, I thought.

After a short visit, I rushed home and put in a call to David Harding. We had to rally the troops, all the former UPI people. John needed us.

David, Lee, and Gene started visiting John, and David and Lee met with me one Saturday after one of my programs at Green Lawn. We talked about John and the progress he was making. It was great seeing some of the old gang again. We had had a few reunions since the breakup started in 1990. David and I had gotten together a few times for lunch or a walk. He got out of journalism all together and went to work as a prison guard. Lee continued in political journalism as the

Statehouse reporter for the *Columbus Dispatch*, leaving UPI a month after I did. We'd kept in touch after he retired, and it was not unusual to get a phone call from him occasionally.

I also got an e-mail from Jim Carter now and then, and he and his wife, Sandy, had joined us for a reunion meal.

Rosemary and I e-mailed about every week. I'd followed her through several jobs—in newspapers in Ohio, Virginia, and Florida, as executive director for Investigative Reporters and Editors, and now at the State University of New York at Albany, her hometown, where she is teaching journalism. When classes are in recess, she teaches investigative reporting in Bosnia. She's become quite a globe-trotter.

It's nice to be able to pick up the phone and call a former colleague and meet for lunch. That's the relationship John and I still have with the people who had worked at UPI. We are family.

One day in 2008 I had a letter from Publish America. I had never heard of this company. And I was nowhere near thinking of writing or publishing a book. I figured I'd open it before throwing it away. I pulled out a news release—John Kady had published a book.

With the news release in one hand, I grabbed the phone with the other and called John at home.

"What's the meaning of this?" I asked. "You published a book? This I gotta see."

We chatted for a while, getting caught up on life since I had last seen him in rehab. While we were talking, I was fishing through my purse for a credit card so I could order his book. I had to see what he was up to. I watched the mail every day like a woman years ago waited for a letter from her loved one. I tore open the package the day it arrived and pulled out the little book *A Sentry's Saga on Okinawa*. It was a fictional story drawn from his experiences in the air police.

As soon as I finished it, I called John and invited him to come to the Ohio Writers Guild with me on Wednesday afternoon. He was hesitant, but he accepted. He called a day or so later, still hesitant about going with me.

"I'm using a walker," he said.

"That doesn't make any difference," I said. "I can handle that."

I've been picking up John nearly every week since that day. He fits right in with this group. We meet weekly, bring in our writing, read it, and critique each other's work.

One thing I have noticed is his short-term memory isn't as sharp as it should be. He'll often ask, "Where do we go?" when we get into the building, or as we leave the elevator to go to the handicapped entrance/exit. I'll always direct him from my car to the handicapped ramp and then meet him at the door to let him in the building.

He was working on another book when we reconnected and soon published *From Kennedy to Kent State: A Reporter's Notebook*.

I was also writing, and in February 2011 I published *Poodle Mistress: The Autobiographical Story of Life with Nine Toy Poodles*.

In the spring of 2009, forty-five people were laid off at the *Columbus Dispatch*. I was one of them. Not long after that I was speaking with a friend who works at the Ohio State Fair for a month in the summer. "How do you get on?" I asked.

The next day I followed her instructions, and now I, too, work at the State Fair in the summer. The first year I worked a month, answering phones and e-mail requests. Now I work during the twelve-day run in an information booth.

UPI is still around, only a shell of its former self. Jay Gibian worked as an assignment editor for a Cleveland TV station and then went back to the new UPI, rewriting stories from releases or newspapers for a while.

There was another bankruptcy. Evangelist Pat Robertson was interested in it, but he said amen and backed away when he realized how deep the debt went. Finally a buyer was found for what was left of it. The Unification Church of the Rev. Sun Myung Moon now owns UPI. But it sure isn't what it used to be.

Meanwhile, I continue to write and keep in touch with other UPI people—via Christmas cards, occasional phone calls, dinner, and e-mail.

In early 2012 I was working on the schedule for the display of photos from the Green Lawn annual photo contest. Some of the entries in the latest contest were from the east side of the county. I wanted to have these photos seen by as many people as possible, so I called the Reynoldsburg Senior Center. The staff had scheduled a tour of Columbus the summer before and was receptive to having the photos on display.

I called David Harding to tell him I was going to be in the area, and we met for coffee the morning I put the photos on display. I would remove them at the end of the month. We made arrangements to meet several others for coffee the day I picked up the photos.

At the end of the month, David and Lee Leonard were available. I took John with me, and the four of us gathered over coffee and pastry at Panera. We nursed our tall cups of coffee for a couple of hours, told stories, and laughed.

As we left the restaurant, one of the young servers—she couldn't have been much over twenty years old—was holding the door for us as we helped John with his walker.

"Would you believe the four of us at that table worked together for twenty years or so more than twenty years ago?" I asked her. "We represent one hundred years of service."

"Oh my gosh!" she exclaimed in amazement.

I tell many people about the closeness the former UPI employees have with their boss. They have a hard time believing me. They tell me they don't even get together with coworkers.

Some former UPI employees started a special service we call Downhold, wire-service speak for holding down expenses. We pass along news about ourselves and others, comment on news stories, or once in a while, share an obituary. I've renewed friendships with people I'd lost touch with after I left and made some new friends.

When Hurricane Sandy blew up the eastern seaboard late in the 2012 hurricane season, the Downhold wire was one way we kept in touch with former employees and how they were affected by that superstorm. Earlier in the summer one message sought travel information. A Downholder was planning a driving vacation through several states. He wanted to know what would be of interest along the way that he should visit. Several of us offered suggestions.

Even though I've been away from UPI since 1990 as a full-time employee and since the spring of 1993 as a once-a-week stringer doing basketball and football scores, it doesn't seem that long ago. I still feel a part of me belongs to UPI, which used to be a bustling wire service.

John and I get together weekly and talk nearly every day on the phone. We are still buddies—and our friendship has lasted longer than many marriages.

"I can't believe when I hired you back then we'd still be together, what is it? Forty years later?" John asked one day while we were waiting for the elevator door to open onto the third floor of the Columbus Cultural Arts Center, where the Ohio Writers Guild meets.

"It's going on forty-five years," I said.

One day in early June 2012, John called.

"David's sick," he said, explaining that he had just gotten off the phone with David Harding. "I asked him, 'What's the matter, David? Flu? Pneumonia?'"

"'I've got pancreatic cancer and am waiting for a visit from hospice," David told John.

"You call people you know," I said. "I'll get on Facebook and search some e-mails I have."

It was a busy afternoon, sending e-mails about David and responding to replies.

A couple of days later, I got an e-mail from Rita Shade of New Jersey, one of the employees who worked with us in the early 1970s and remained a friend with David.

"What should I do?" she asked. I advised a phone call, then possibly a cheery letter.

She said she'd call. A short time later I received another e-mail that she was too late with the call. A friend of his answered the phone and advised her that David had passed away during the night. It had been ten days since his diagnosis, and now we were facing a funeral.

A short time later I walked into the living room, where my husband, now long retired, was watching TV.

"David's dead," I said, letting the tears fall.

"You have to notify Rosemary and Mason," were his first words.

"I sent Rosemary and some others an e-mail, and here," I said, waving a folded sheet of paper I was putting into an envelope, "is a letter to Mason."

"He didn't look sick when he was out here not long ago," Red said.

David had come out to pick me up, and we went over to get John and take him to Beulah Park for horse racing around Kentucky Derby time. Beulah wasn't running live ponies that day, so we watched a few simulcast races.

Red and David began talking about cars. David was driving a convertible; he'd had convertibles for a long time. Red was showing off his Lincoln MKX SUV.

Now the e-mails and phone calls among many of us aren't quite as chipper as they once had been.

"Someone has to represent UPI," said Jim Sielicki. As UPI was going down, he did stints in Washington and Detroit, and is now working for the *Toledo Blade*, where the editor is another UPI alum out of Columbus.

John and I drove up to Lima, ninety miles northwest of Columbus, for David's funeral. Meeting us at the funeral home was Jim Sielicki.

That gathering prompted serious work on a get-together. John started calling around to find a restaurant that had a meeting room we could use. Some of us had come together in a restaurant one evening, but we were in the midst of regular diners and had a tendency to get loud. I wanted to be off to ourselves, where our laughter wouldn't interrupt others.

John thought nothing of picking up the phone and calling people who had worked for and with him over the years and inviting them to dinner. Throughout this process, we reconnected with many people who have UPI/Columbus in their résumé.

The gang is still mostly intact. Granted, we've lost a few: Dick Lightner, Dick Wheeler, Dan Crawford, Jay Gibian, David Harding, and Mason Blosser. The older operators have all passed on too. But most of us are still newsroom buddies and have been for a good forty-five years. We've been through the good and the bad; we've had our ups and our downs. We often likened it to a marriage, but none of us have had a marriage (yet) as long as our friendship.

Chapter 60

Sandi
August 29, 2013
John T. Kady
September 2, 1933–August 4, 2013
-30-

In mid-2013 I was determined to get this work finished and to the publisher. I reverted to my trusty hour-a-day plan to do the editing. I was even working on a time frame and had a date in mind to start sending this to the publisher.

As with all the best plans, something is bound to happen. I had an unexpected visit from Ms. Murphy of Murphy's Law.

The first stumbling block came during the Ohio State Fair in late July. I was to work a six-hour shift as a guest information specialist in the information booth at the Ohio Gate during the twelve-day run. I've done this for several years. Only this year, a worker hired for an evening shift at one of the other booths didn't report for her position, and another guest information specialist and I alternated working that second shift to cover that booth. I worked six hours one day and eleven hours within a twelve-hour day the next for the entire run.

I didn't get any editing done. I figured I had a few days between the

State Fair and going to Salt Lake City on August 21 for the National Federation of Press Women conference.

The Monday after the State Fair I was cleaning off my voice mail on my landline when I came to a message from Patti Kady. She had left it the day before, Sunday, August 4.

"Jack passed away this morning," she said. Only Patti called John by the nickname Jack.

John had been in Franklin Woods Rehabilitation Center since spring. He had fallen three times one weekend at home and it was too much for Patti to get him up, so she had called the emergency squad each time.

I had talked with John Saturday morning before I started my day's work. He had told me he had pneumonia but wanted to get help in locating some former employees so we could invite them to a UPI get-together.

"John, I'm working at the State Fair for another two days. I'll talk with you about it when I get done there," I said, thinking now that I was a little sharp with him.

After getting the voice mail, I checked in on Downhold and started notifying former coworkers and our writing friends about John's passing.

Condolences started pouring in. One response was "Crap!" Another read, "Bad news." Some were the expected: "My condolences to the family" or "He will be missed."

From Margie Hiermer from our writing group, the Ohio Writers Guild: "My deepest condolences to you and John's family. Thank you for sending this to all of us. John was indeed an American original, but then you know that well. Between you and me, I'll never forget the day in Guild he asked me if I ever smoked pot in a bong with wine in it. Then he punctuated the question with, 'Well, it gets you really screwed up.' Just loved that guy."

Don Mullen, who had worked on UPI's general desk in New York, remembered him as "really great to work with. He was always up and at 'em, with a great sense of humor. The National Desk could always depend on him to get his skeds in on time and back them up with solid, play-winning stories."

The sked is an item sent to clients at the top of each cycle, whether it is for morning or afternoon papers, advising editors what stories will be coming, the author, the approximate length of the story, and if a new lead is expected.

As for John's humor, Tom Burnett, who worked in the Columbus and Cleveland offices in the 1980s and 1990s, remembered "one election night, everyone would work, and John would often bring the staffers from one-person bureaus to Columbus to better coordinate coverage and stories. One of them was Mary Kane (who I believe is now with Newhouse's Washington bureau). Anyway, at this time she was in her midtwenties and looked ten years younger and had been assigned to the Dayton bureau. Pizza was ordered for the staff that night. Mary goes back to work in Dayton and on Friday gets a business-sized envelope from Columbus, opens it up, and it's a congealed slice of pizza wrapped in copy paper with a note from John: 'You forgot this the other night.'"

John always called himself "the world's greatest desk man," and Burnett summed it up pretty well:

> John's real talent was as a rewrite man. For those not in the business, a rewrite person is someone who takes dictation from an on-the-scene reporter and fashions it into what the reader sees. They were the literally unsung heroes at UPI because the byline would always go to the reporter. In many cases with John, what I'd give him over the phone would be random notes and quotes and observations that were in no way in any coherent order. Give him a few minutes, and he'd get a well-written piece on the wire ... If some client mentioned to him, "Hey, that was a great story by (reporter)," he'd never say, "I wrote it."

Some of his hires remembered him for giving them a chance.

Rich Exner of the *Cleveland Plain Dealer* posted on Facebook: "Great guy John Kady, and the guy who took a chance on an 'Ohio Valley' kid—me—who had not yet graduated from OSU when he hired me at UPI in 1985."

The same sentiment came from Tim Miller, now at Fahlgren

advertising agency after stints at UPI and the *Dayton Daily News*: "John took a chance on this kid from Perry County, too, and my life was never the same."

That was similar to the way I got my job. John called me in Delaware when I was on the streets meeting the newsmakers and looking for news stories and put me on the Ohio UPI broadcast desk.

John often told the story of a young woman who came in to the office one day, soaking wet after having been caught in an afternoon pop-up shower, common in central Ohio. She had been turned down at both the *Columbus Dispatch* and the *Columbus Citizen-Journal* because she didn't have any experience.

"She stood there, hands on her hips, and said, 'Mr. Kady, how can I get experience if no one will hire me?'"

John hired her on the spot. Betsy Neus turned out to be a gold nugget. Today she is in a high leadership role at Gannett in Washington.

Although John grew up around racehorses, he also loved football, especially the Ohio State Buckeyes. He often went to the games as a second sportswriter for UPI. At times he'd send a young reporter to get the feel of how coverage was to be done.

One time when he sent a young reporter, the two were talking on the phone before the game. John was telling the reporter how to write the story. The reporter was making notes and repeating them out loud.

"In the background I could hear someone saying, 'And you'd better do as Mr. Kady tells you,'" John related.

John had requested that in lieu of flowers, memorials should be sent to Thoroughbred Retirement Foundation, which is dedicated to the rescue and retirement of aged racehorses.

Said Chris Graham: "I love the idea that he requested remembrances be sent to a group that helps out tired, old racehorses. Only John would think of that. Another reason he was a most interesting member of this human community."

I compiled all the condolences and took them over to Patti. We also discussed the progress on this book. "What do I do now?" was my main question.

"Is the writing all done?" she asked.

"Yes," I replied. "I'm in the final stages of editing."

We decided that I'd finish the editing and proceed with what John and I had talked about.

Ten former UPI employees and spouses were in the congregation for John's memorial Mass.

Celebrant Father Homer Blubaugh had John pegged right when he said John always had a story. He even quoted one light area from John's book *From Kennedy to Kent State*—the part where then Sen. Kennedy was questioning Cardinal Spellman about what the Pope would say about his being a leader of the country. And Cardinal Spellman said, "I don't know, Jack. He still calls me Spillman."

One of John's brothers said the T., his middle initial, stood for trouble. He then told the story of Jack (the name the family called him) being invited to a birthday party at the age of two and beating up on the other guests.

Another of John's brothers made a pitch for the congregation to buy his book, while brother Marty sang "My Way" with special lyrics, inserting Jack wherever possible.

Former UPI employees collected money to send a bouquet of flowers with a ribbon that said -30-. Daughter Gretchen said she and Jennifer often got into trouble in school when they put -30- at the end of their homework.

The most common story of -30- dates back to the Civil War, when correspondents were sending their stories by telegraph. An X would stand for a period, XX would stand for a paragraph, and XXX for the end of the story. XXX in Roman numerals is -30-.

John always signed off jtk, showing who wrote the story. Thursday, August 29, 2013, we said -30- to John.

Appendix

Here are recipes for some of the food Sandi used to bring in to UPI.

Swedish Meatballs

1 pint sour cream
1 package dehydrated onion soup mix
1 cup milk

1 1/2 pounds ground beef
1 1/2 cups soft bread crumbs (or cracker crumbs)
1 egg, beaten
1/4 teaspoon allspice
1/2 teaspoon nutmeg

butter (optional)

Blend together sour cream and onion soup mix.

In another bowl, combine 1 cup of the sour cream/onion soup mixture with the meat, bread (or cracker) crumbs, beaten egg, and spices. Mix thoroughly and form into balls. Roll in flour.

Stir the milk with the remaining sour cream and onion soup mix.

In a large skillet, melt 2 tablespoons butter and brown the meatballs. Or brown them in a microwaveable pan that allows the fat to drain into a drip pan to be tossed out.

Put meatballs into a large sauce pan and add the soup-mix liquid and heat through. Or put the meatballs in a microwaveable bowl, add the soup-mix liquid, and heat through.

Serving suggestion: Serve over hot noodles or rice.

Submitted to the *Columbus Dispatch* in 1970 by Mrs. Delma K. Jackson with my own instructions for microwave ovens.

Apple Cream Pie

Filling:
1 envelope unflavored gelatin
2/3 cup sugar
2/3 cup apple juice

2 three-ounce packages cream cheese
1 tablespoon lemon juice
2 medium apples
1/2 cup whipping cream (or 8-oz. Cool Whip)
1 graham cracker crust pie

Mix gelatin, sugar, and apple juice, stirring constantly over medium heat until gelatin is dissolved. Refrigerate until thick.

Beat 2 three-ounce packages cream cheese and 1 tablespoon lemon juice in small mixer bowl. Add the thickened gelatin mixture; beat until smooth, about one minute. Refrigerate until thick.

Pare, core, and finely chop two medium apples into gelatin/cheese mixture.

Fold in 1/2 cup whipping cream, whipped (or 8-oz. container Cool Whip).

Pour into crust. Refrigerate a couple of hours before cutting.

Found in a cooking magazine in the early 1970s. I can't remember the name of the magazine, and it didn't last very long.

Daffodil Cake

1 cup sifted cake flour
1 1/4 cup sifted sugar
1 cup egg whites (at room temperature)
1 teaspoon cream of tartar
1/4 teaspoon salt
1/2 teaspoon vanilla
1 teaspoon grated orange rind
2 tablespoons orange juice
4 egg yolks

Sift flour once, measure, add 1/2 cup of sugar, and sift together four times.

Beat egg whites and salt. When foamy, add cream of tartar and continue beating until eggs are stiff enough to hold up in peaks, but not dry.

Add remaining sugar, 2 tablespoons at a time, beating after each addition until sugar is just blended.

Sift a small amount of flour over mixture and fold in lightly. Repeat until all is used.

Divide batter in two parts.

To one, fold in vanilla.

To the other, add orange rind and juice and 2 additional tablespoons sugar to egg yolks; beat until very thick and light.

Spoon mixtures into an ungreased round 10-inch tube pan, alternating yellow and white. (Pan should be half full.)

Bake in moderate oven (375 degrees) for 30 minutes or until done.

Remove from oven, invert pan, and let stand one hour or until cake is cool.

From Louise Augenstein, Crawford County home economist in the 1950s.

Pumpkin Bread

1 cup sugar
2 eggs
1 cup pumpkin
3/4 cup cooking oil
1 1/2 cup flour
1 teaspoon baking powder
1 teaspoon soda
1 teaspoon nutmeg
1 teaspoon cinnamon
1/4 teaspoon salt
1 1/2 cup chopped nuts

Mix together sugar, pumpkin, eggs; add oil.
Gradually add dry ingredients.
Stir in nuts last.
Bake in well-greased loaf pan at 350 degrees for one hour.

Can also be baked as muffins by filling cupcake liners. Bake for 20 minutes or until a toothpick inserted comes out clean.

From Carolyn Dill Barnes, Delaware County home economist in late 1960s.